COUNTERKNOWLEDGE

...ian Thompson completed his PhD in the sociology of
...gion at the London School of Economics. He is a leader
...iter for the *Daily Telegraph*. He is also editor-in-chief of
... *Catholic Herald*, and the author of *The End of Time* (1996)
...d *Waiting for Antichrist* (2005).

...hat's not to like? This book looks cool. It fires a breezily
...bust missile into the bellies of pseudo history, health
...ackery, creationism, the 9/11 Truth movement and the
...doubtable "Dr" Gillian McKeith. It seems a perfect little
... oste to the cultic milieu in which we suddenly, somehow,
...pear to have found ourselves . . . As a contemporary paean
... reason, *Counterknowledge* is a reassurance to those of us
...strated by friends sending sinister jpegs of a post-9/11
...ntagon, but who could never quite deconstruct their dodgy
... on. Now we can counter the counterknowledge.'

Pol Ò Conghaile, *Irish Examiner*

COUNTERKNOWLEDGE

How we surrendered to
conspiracy theories, quack medicine,
bogus science and fake history

DAMIAN THOMPSON

Atlantic Books

London

First published in hardback in Great Britain in 2008 by Atlantic Books,
an imprint of Grove/Atlantic Ltd.

This paperback edition published in Great Britain in 2008 by Atlantic Books.

1 2 3 4 5 6 7 8 9

A CIP catalogue record for this book is available
from the British Library.

ISBN: 978 1 84354 676 4

Typeset in Palatino by Ellipsis Books Limited, Glasgow

Printed in Great Britain by CPI Bookmarque, Croydon, CR0 4TD

Atlantic Books
An imprint of Grove Atlantic Ltd
Ormond House
26–27 Boswell Street
London
WC1N 3JZ

www.atlantic-books.co.uk

For Carmel

Contents

Acknowledgements

I am very lucky to be represented by Simon Trewin, who put me in touch with Toby Mundy of Atlantic Books, the most inspiring editor I have ever worked with. I would also like to thank Emma Grove for her advice and moral support. Angus Broadbent and Igor Toronyi-Lalic read early drafts of chapters and told me that I could do better: they were right. My dear friends Luke Coppen, Stephen Hough and Harry Mount egged me on; Milo Andreas Wagner expertly identified problems of style and structure, and also created a website, www.counterknowledge.com, where bloggers can join the fights I have picked in this book. I'm very much in his debt. Ben Goldacre, arch tormentor of scientific snake oil salesmen, generously supplied me with extra ammunition. Finally, I will always be grateful to the crime novelist Stav Sherez, who came up with the word 'counterknowledge'. Why didn't I think of that?

1

Knowledge and Counterknowledge

The US government knew in advance about the plan to crash passenger jets into the World Trade Center. There is a link between childhood autism and the MMR triple vaccine against measles, mumps and rubella. A Chinese fleet circumnavigated the globe in the early fifteenth century, reaching America seventy years before Columbus. The structure of a cell is too complex to have evolved through natural selection.

All four of these statements have been presented as fact by reputable publishing houses, discussed respectfully by newspaper columnists, quoted by politicians and circulated on the internet. Tens of millions of people believe them to be true. Yet all four are false – that is, factually incorrect.

This is counterknowledge: misinformation packaged to look like fact – packaged so effectively, indeed, that the twenty-first century is facing a pandemic of credulous thinking. Ideas that, in their original, raw form, flourished only on the fringes of society are now being taken seriously by educated people in the West, and are circulating with bewildering speed in the developing world.

We are lucky to live in an age in which the techniques available for evaluating the truth or falsehood of claims about science and history are more reliable than ever before. Yet, disturbingly, we are witnessing a huge surge in the popularity of propositions that fail basic empirical tests. The essence of counterknowledge is that it purports to be knowledge but is *not* knowledge. Its claims can be shown to be untrue, either because there are facts that contradict them or because there is no evidence to support them. It misrepresents reality (deliberately or otherwise) by presenting non-facts as facts.

Obviously, only claims about the material world can be demolished empirically. Many religious doctrines, by their nature, cannot be tested by the evidence of our senses and therefore do not fit neatly into the category of counterknowledge, however preposterous they may be. Science cannot tell us whether God exists or whether there is such a thing as reincarnation. Religion enters the realm of counterknowledge only when it makes factually incorrect statements – which certain religions, such as fundamentalist Christianity and Islam, do with alarming frequency. Creationists, for example, spend most of their time dismissing the overwhelming scientific evidence showing that all life evolved through natural processes of random mutation and selection. But when they do make testable claims of their own – for example, that there was a world-wide flood about 4,000 years ago – they are shown to be utterly false.[1]

One of the greatest legacies of the European Enlightenment is a scientific methodology that allows us to make increasingly accurate observations about the world around us. This methodology is based on the assumption that all we need in order to comprehend nature is a solid understanding of the laws and processes that we can observe and test in the natural world. The supernatural does not enter the equation, because it does not provide us with any explanations that can be tested empirically.[2]

That legacy is now threatened. And one of the reasons for this, paradoxically, is that science has given us almost unlimited access to fake information.

Some bogus material is easily spotted: its theories are clearly outlandish and the individuals who champion them are dishonest or gullible. Most of us have acquaintances who are susceptible to conspiracy theories. You may know someone who thinks the churches are suppressing the truth that Jesus and Mary Magdalene sired a dynasty of Merovingian kings; someone else who thinks AIDS was invented in a CIA laboratory; someone else again who thinks MI5 had a hand in the death of Diana, Princess of Wales. Perhaps you know one person who believes all three.

Or do you at least half-believe one of them yourself?

We may tell ourselves that only oddballs subscribe to bogus history and bogus science. We assume that we ourselves are immune to the false logic of the conspiracy theory. In reality, we are more vulnerable to it than at any time for decades.

I was at a dinner party recently where a Liberal Democrat-voting schoolteacher voiced his 'doubts' about 9/11. First, he grabbed our attention with a plausible-sounding observation: 'Look at the way the towers collapsed vertically, instead of toppling over. Jet fuel wouldn't generate enough to heat to melt steel. Only controlled explosions can do that.' The other guests, not being professional structural engineers (for whom there is nothing mysterious about the collapse of the towers) pricked up their ears. 'How fascinating!' they said. 'You're right, it did seem strange . . .'

For an awful moment, it looked as if the teacher had won some converts. But then, fortunately, one or two guests thought more carefully what they were being asked to believe. If there was a controlled explosion, then the American authorities helped murder thousands of US citizens. Why? The people at the dinner party disliked George W. Bush, but they didn't think he was a James Bond villain. The Lib Dem teacher switched tack and wheeled out the 'fact' (also circulated by the former British government minister Michael Meacher, MP) that the US Air Force stood down its fighter jets that morning. But another guest had read an article exposing this claim as rubbish. The air force did not 'stand down' its jets, he explained; but it could not intercept the hijacked planes because the terrorists had turned off the transponders that would have allowed ground radar to pick out the planes from the 4,500 in US air space at that moment.[3] The audience turned against the teacher, who ended up stumbling pathetically down a rhetorical escape route: 'I'm just saying that we shouldn't believe everything we are told.'

On this occasion, the 9/11 'expert' did not persuade his audience. Unfortunately, more and more fantasists are succeeding where he failed. It's true that no major newspaper or TV station in Britain or America has officially endorsed a 9/11 conspiracy theory; indeed, in February 2007, a BBC documentary shown on terrestrial television went through the alternative scenarios in detail and concluded that none of them could actually have happened.[4] But the mainstream media are fast losing their grip on public opinion.

In May 2006, a ninety-minute documentary about 9/11 called *Loose Change* reached the number-one slot on Google Video. The film has been accessed over six million times on that site alone and has been posted in many different edited versions on YouTube. It is streamed online in seven foreign languages and sold as a DVD. The directors claim that 100 million people worldwide have seen it.[5]

The original half-hour cut of *Loose Change* was put

together by three young New York film-makers – Dylan Avery, Korey Rowe and Jason Bermas – on a laptop computer. The budget for the 2006 full-length version was a mere $6,000. Yet the result is super-slick: computer-generated planes glide menacingly towards their targets, to the accompaniment of a funky soundtrack; buildings collapse in a comic theatrical sequence while Avery asks pointed questions in a laid-back tone. This is one cool movie – and a masterpiece of counterknowledge.

The makers of *Loose Change* believe that the US government was behind 9/11. In support of this conclusion, they suggest that a missile, not an airliner, hit the Pentagon; that the occupants of Flight 93 were safely evacuated at Cleveland Hopkins airport; that the cellphone calls made by the passengers before it crashed were faked using voice-morphing technology; that the Twin Towers and the nearby World Trade Center 7 building (which fell down as the result of a fire) were brought down by controlled explosions.

In the course of advancing their thesis, the directors make the most basic errors and play outrageous tricks: quotes from experts and official documents are cherry-picked and truncated to eradicate information that contradicts the conspiracy theory. So, for example, Marcel Bernard, the flight instructor of Hani Hanjour, who flew Flight 77 into the Pentagon, is interviewed talking about his pupil's poor flying skills. The impression is that Bernard, like the film-makers, believes that Hanjour did not have the ability to pilot the plane towards the building. In fact, Bernard is on record as saying the opposite, but we are never told this. Likewise, we hear a quote from Danielle O'Brien, an air traffic controller at Washington's Dulles Airport saying that she and her colleagues thought Flight 77 was a military aircraft; but we never hear the next sentence, in which she explains that the reason they thought this was because it was performing manoeuvres that were 'unsafe' for a Boeing 757.

The photographic evidence offered by *Loose Change* is equally unreliable; aircraft parts are misidentified and pictures cropped in a way that leaves out inconvenient sections of rubble and wreckage. Experts who accept the official version of events (who include every major demolition firm in the world) are never interviewed; meanwhile, much of the 'expert testimony' that supports the film's thesis is lifted from the American Free Press (AFP), a hysterically anti-Zionist news service which has strong links to far right groups and blames American school shootings on teaching children about the Holocaust.[6] The AFP shares a postal address with, and provides a link to, the neo-Nazi magazine the *Barnes Review*, which in August 2007 was advertising a book called *The Myth of the Six Million* by David Hoggan.[7] *Loose Change* cites the AFP several times – for example, on the claim that an engine part found in the Pentagon crash site did not belong to a

Boeing 757. (It later turned out that the AFP reporter had called the wrong aircraft factory by mistake.[8])

The absurdity of the conspiracy theory espoused by the *Loose Change* team has appalled even left-wing commentators. As Matt Taibbi observed on his *Rolling Stone* blog in September 2006: 'I have no doubt that every time one of those *Loose Change* dickwads opens his mouth, a Republican somewhere picks up five votes.'[9] Maybe so, but the *Loose Change* bandwagon seems virtually unstoppable.

In May 2007 it was announced that the rights to the film had been acquired by the production company Revolver; the third and final cut was scheduled for UK cinema release later in the year.[10] Meanwhile, the film's allegations, none of which bears close examination, have been repeated by airhead celebrities, including the ABC talk-show host Rosie O'Donnell, who was filmed on a cellphone warming up her studio audience by suggesting that the official explanation for the collapse of WTC 7 was 'impossible, physics-wise'.[11]

O'Donnell described her views as 'hard to say in America' – that is, unacceptable to the media and public opinion. She may be right about the media, but the proportion of the American public that believes that the Bush administration was complicit in 9/11 is astonishingly high. According to a 2006 Scripps Howard poll, most young Americans and more than a third (36 per cent) of the adult population of the United States suspect that federal officials assisted in the 9/11 attacks or deliberately took no action to stop them, so that the United States could go to war in the Middle East.[12]

Meanwhile, 9/11 conspiracy theories have gained such a following in France that even a minister in President Nicolas Sarkozy's government has suggested that President Bush might have planned the terror attacks. Christine Boutin, the French housing minister, was asked in an interview in November 2006 (before she took office) whether she thought Bush might have been behind the attacks. 'I think it is possible. I think it is possible,' she replied. Her reasoning? 'I know that the websites that speak of this problem are websites that have the highest number of visits,' she said. 'And I tell myself that this expression of the masses and of the people cannot be without any truth.'[13]

Someone else who believes this is Mahmoud Ahmadinejad, the president of Iran, who in 2006 wrote an open letter to President Bush suggesting that 9/11 could not have been planned and executed 'without coordination with [US] intelligence and security services'.[14] This letter was then picked up by Western conspiracy websites and quoted as evidence that the head of state of a major country shared their suspicions.[15] We do not know whether Ahmadinejad has seen *Loose Change*, but he is certainly a fan of one of the film's main sources, the American Free Press, whose correspondent Michael Collins Piper he invited to Iran for an exclusive interview. (Piper duly found him 'witty, whip-smart and spiritual . . . a firm voice against the forces that demand submission to a New World Order'.[16])

Ahmadinejad is also a well-known Holocaust denier, having referred publicly to 'the myth of the Jews' massacre'.[17] The fact that he combines this stance with 9/11 scepticism is no great surprise. While most 9/11 conspiracy theorists are not anti-Semites, there is an overlap between the two constituencies. To give just one example, a website called Serendipity.li, which claims to have been the first to put forward the *Loose Change* thesis that the World Trade Center was demolished by controlled explosions, also posted an article marking the names of Jews in the Bush administration with Nazi-style yellow stars.[18]

This overlap should not surprise us. As the editor of *Skeptic* magazine, Michael Shermer, wrote in *Scientific American*, 'the mistaken belief that a handful of unexplained anomalies can undermine a well-established theory lies at the heart of all conspiratorial thinking (as well as Creationism, Holocaust denial and the various crank theories of physics). All the "evidence" for a 9/11 conspiracy falls under this rubric.'[19]

We do not normally think of Creationism and maverick physics as conspiracy theories; but what they have in common with *Loose Change* is a methodology – or a lack of one – that marks them out as categories of counterknowledge. People who share a muddled, careless or deceitful attitude towards gathering evidence often find themselves drawn to each other's fantasies. If you believe one wrong or strange thing, you are more likely to believe another.

For centuries, unorthodox beliefs – that is, beliefs rejected by the guardians of intellectual orthodoxy – have tended to cling together. This tendency was observable long before society developed a scientific methodology that enabled it to distinguish between true and false empirical claims. In an article about the origins of the New Age movement, the American sociologist Robert Ellwood described an 'underground river' of alternative spirituality dating back to the ancient Greeks, which became visible in the forms of Renaissance occultism, Freemasonry, Spiritualism and Theosophy.[20] In many of these movements, belief in one doctrine rejected by society led to another. Late medieval sects, for example, might combine unorthodox interpretation of the Bible with mystical healing ceremonies or forbidden sexual practices.

As Western knowledge became more systematic and evidence-based, ideas that failed the new intellectual tests were increasingly banished to the fringes of society, where they exhibited a magnetic attraction towards one another. By the middle of the nineteenth century, a pamphlet written by a freelance prophet or spiritual guru would typically offer the public a whole smorgasbord of bizarre ideas. I have on my bookshelf a huge annotated bibliography of doomsday tracts. The other day I opened it at random. The first publication I came across was entitled *Armageddon; or, The Overthrow of Romanism and Monarchy*, by Samuel Davies Baldwin, published in Cincinnati in 1854. It reveals that Armageddon will be fought on American soil; that the Semites are an inferior 'yellow' race; that the numerical values of the word 'Latinos' add up to 666; that archaeological remains of a Lost Tribe of Israel can be found in the Midwest; and that the proof that Americans are the chosen people is that the number of Christians in America in 1776, 144,000, precisely matched the number of the saved in the Book of Revelation.[21]

This ingenious synthesis of apocalyptic prophecy, bogus archaeology, numerology and racism is an early product of what the sociologist Colin Campbell calls the 'cultic milieu'.[22] This term, coined in the 1970s, refers to a cultural space in which, in effect, anything goes: strange ideas mix and merge, unrestricted by conventional rules of evidence.

The cultic milieu makes room for the 9/11 theories, Creationism, Holocaust denial and crank physics mentioned by Shermer; to this list we can add belief in UFOs, astrology, ESP, near-death experiences, miracle diets and Bible prophecy. The fact that all these ideas are, to a greater or lesser extent, stigmatized by the Establishment is a crucial part of their appeal. A single countercultural belief is a passport to a thrilling alternative universe in which Atlantis is buried underneath the Antarctic, the Ark of the Covenant is hidden in Ethiopia, aliens have manipulated our DNA, and there was once a civilization on Mars. (All these theories, incidentally, have been put forward by just one author, Graham Hancock, who was taken seriously enough as an 'alternative archaeologist' to be given his own television series on Channel 4 in 1998.)

The surreal quality of the cultic milieu was brought home to me in 1996 when I visited Japan to write about Aum Shinrikyo, the apocalyptic sect that tried to jump-start Armageddon by releasing sarin gas on the Tokyo underground. The sect believed in reincarnation, 'earthquake weapons', UFOs, Masonic conspiracies – and, I was surprised to discover, the prophecies of St Malachy. In 1139, this Bishop of Armagh is supposed to have received a glimpse of every future pope until the end of the world, each identified by a cryptic nickname. John Paul II was *De Labore Solis* ('of the work of the Sun'), to be followed by *Gloria Olivae* ('the glory of the olive'), and then *Petrus Romanus*, the final successor of St Peter. 'So it will be approximately twenty years to the end of the last pope,' explained Shoko Asahara, the half-blind madman who founded Aum Shinrikyo.

The prophecies are bogus. The nicknames of the popes who lived before the list was 'discovered' (that is, forged) in about 1590 are uncannily apt, while thereafter they are cunningly vague. What startled me was the realization that the last person to reveal the secrets of St Malachy to me was my beloved grandmother. In other words, the same strand of misinformation had found its way almost simultaneously to a terraced house in Blackpool and a cult compound on the slopes of Mount Fuji. It is hard to imagine a better demonstration of the vigour of the cultic milieu.

Now, thanks to the internet, the milieu is positively buzzing: a rumour about the Antichrist can leap from Goths in Sweden to an extreme traditionalist Catholic sect in Australia in a matter of seconds. Minority groups are becoming ever more tolerant of each other's eccentric doctrines. Contacts between white and black racists, which began tentatively decades ago, are now flourishing as the two groups swap conspiracy stories. In particular, the growing anti-Semitism of black American Muslims has proved to be a great ice-breaker on the neo-Nazi circuit.[23] In June 2007, the home page of The Truth Seeker, a conspiracy website, included claims that AIDS is a 'man-made Pentagon genocide', that Pope Paul VI 'was impersonated by an actor from 1975 to 1978', that new evidence of the Loch Ness monster has emerged – plus a link to *Loose Change*.[24]

But can a film whose central claim is broadly accepted by a third of Americans really be classified as belonging to a deluded fringe? The term 'cultic milieu' is less useful than it used to be because it is too restrictive. In the twenty-first century, bogus knowledge is no longer mainly confined to self-selecting minority groups. It is seeping from the cultic milieu into the mainstream, cleverly repackaged for an international mass market.

That sounds rather like a conspiracy theory, so I should stress that I don't think there is a massive, concerted campaign to feed lies to the public. One of the distinguishing features of counterknowledge is a casual approach to the truth: it encourages and takes advantage of a significant lowering of the standards of proof in society generally. As a result, we are exposed to all sorts of empirically dubious information, much of it conceived in a spirit of credulity or carelessness rather than actual deceit. So we should be careful before using the word 'lie'. As the Princeton philosopher Harry Frankfurt points out in his marvellous essay 'On Bullshit', 'it is impossible for someone to lie unless he knows the truth'.[25]

Some purveyors of counterknowledge – Creationists, for example – believe passionately that their misrepresentation of empirical data conveys the truth. Others fit Frankfurt's description of the bullshitter: 'He does not care whether the things he says describe reality correctly. He just picks them out, or makes them up, to suit his purpose.'[26] And, of course, there are barefaced liars who know that they are guilty of deception; but you could argue that these people are less dangerous than totally deluded ones, or people who play intellectual tricks in the service of a bizarre belief system in which they at least intermittently believe.

In the end, the motives of the producers of dubious material are less important than the truth of their claims. The essence of counterknowledge is that its factual claims can be shown to be wrong. I say 'shown' rather than 'proven' because, in science, observable facts do not 'prove' a theory: they render it probable to some degree.

The difference between a false and a true theory is one of probability. For example, hard-line Creationists believe that the world is a few thousand years old; geologists believe it is a few billion years old. We can say with confidence that the latter theory is true because there is a mountain of evidence supporting it. We can also say, with even greater confidence, that the 'young earth' theory is false, because the evidence offered in support of it is so laughably feeble as to be non-existent. We do not need an alternative explanation to knock down a false belief; if there are no facts making a claim even slightly probable, then it is false.[27]

Ideas are counterknowledge only if they run counter to real knowledge. For that reason, it is unwise to apply the word to heterodox claims made before the twentieth century. Until then, academic methodology was a very hit-and-miss affair. Some of the most rigorous thinkers of the sixteenth and seventeenth centuries believed in flying witches. Sir Isaac Newton thought his discovery of calculus was just as scientific as his attempt to extract the date of the Second Coming from clues in the Book of Daniel, which is nowadays the sort of project we associate with the more desperate breed of televangelist.

Obviously, there was no single moment at which scientists could say: 'Now we know more or less how the physical universe works.' Arguably, we still haven't reached that point, since (for example) the study of quantum physics and the human brain is still in its infancy. But we *do* have a methodology, which reached maturity during the last century, for evaluating the probability of claims relating exclusively to the material, measurable world. And the essence of this methodology is our ability to show that a particular proposition is false – that is, that there are no data making it probable. As the philosopher Sir Karl Popper argued, theories become science only when they have survived our most brutal attempts to falsify them. We cannot infer the truth of a theory by observation, but we can demolish it by observing facts that run counter to it or by showing that no facts support it.[28]

Before we brand something as counterknowledge, therefore, we must be able to demonstrate that its propositions are factually incorrect. In many cases, this is not as difficult as it sounds, because the propositions of conspiracy theorists, amateur archaeologists, miracle-working gurus et al. are so obviously ridiculous. They can be knocked down using basic statistics, elementary logic or a Google search – though be careful about that last one.

Just as we know that the earth is not 6,000 years old,

we can be sure that crystals do not possess energy capable of healing physical ailments; that aliens did not land at Roswell; that the sun did not spin in the sky during the reported apparitions of the Virgin Mary at Fatima, Portugal, in 1917. These come into the category of propositions you could stake your life on being untrue, thanks to overwhelming evidence contradicting them or a decisive absence of evidence pointing in their favour.

Pedlars of counterknowledge often insist that their ideas should be taken seriously because 'no one has been able to come up with a better explanation' for whatever mystery they have lighted upon. But this argument only betrays their muddled thinking. The fact that a subject is genuinely puzzling, that there are vast gaps in our understanding of it, does not lower the standard of evidence we require in order to fill in the gaps. We do not need to master the intricacies of Mayan cosmology (which no one yet has) to know that it did not anticipate the Pacific tsunami of 26 December 2004, as the amateur archaeologist Adrian Gilbert suggests.[29] We do not need to have unravelled the mysteries of quantum mechanics (something no physicist would claim to have done) to know that cancer patients who overcome their illness have not made a literal 'quantum jump', as the New Age medical guru Deepak Chopra ludicrously claims.[30]

Moreover, you do not need to be 99.9999 per cent certain that a claim is false to label it as counterknowledge. Some bogus ideas are a bit less improbable than the ones listed above – and, as a result, it is easier to make them sound plausible. It is just conceivable that documents will come to light suggesting that Jesus and Mary Magdalene married and moved to France; that the Protocols of the Elders of Zion describe a real Jewish conspiracy; that President Bush knew in advance about the attack on the Twin Towers. Conceivable – but fantastically unlikely. Yet the international market for all three of these fatuous propositions grew substantially in the years 2002–7, thanks to popular books and films that advanced them.

And that brings us back to the depressing paradox I described at the beginning of this chapter. At a time when our techniques for evaluating evidence are subtler than ever before, counterknowledge is not only fooling the public but also corrupting intellectual standards across a range of disciplines.

Almost every big social change of the last thirty years has contributed to the accretion of counterknowledge. There is the explosive growth in the variety and reach of the media, especially the internet; the effect of free-market capitalism on the way we interpret information and choose beliefs; the painful integration of developing countries into the global economy; mass migration to the West; and the rise of fundamentalist Islam.

The media were pushing the circulation of counterknowledge long before the public hooked up to broadband. Consider, for example, the satanic ritual abuse (SRA) scare of the 1980s and 1990s. In the early 1980s, American evangelical Christians started reporting stories of satanists who impregnated women ('brood mares') so they could eat their babies; no one is quite sure where these stories originated. Then they spread to the whole English-speaking world.

The panic-mongers in this wretched saga included radical feminists, social workers and fundamentalist Christians, all of whom had their own reasons for wanting the stories to be true. For feminists, SRA was the ultimate expression of male domination; for social workers, it was an exciting opportunity to rush around 'diagnosing' abuse and removing children into care; for fundamentalists, it was a manifestation of the flourishing of worldwide evil before the coming of the Antichrist.

But the SRA scare would have got nowhere without the media. In 1987, in the first of a series of special reports, US talk-show host Geraldo Rivera announced: 'Experts estimate there are over one million satanists in this country ... From small towns to large cities, they have attracted police and FBI attention to their satanic ritual child abuse, child pornography and satanic murders. The odds are that this is happening in your town.'[31] In his book, *Satanic Panic*, the sociologist Jeffrey Victor shows how the Rivera broadcasts, together with panic-stricken coverage by regional television stations and newspapers, created local epidemics of rumours; he even provides a map to show how panic about devil-worship swept through a group of small towns in upper New York state in 1988.[32]

In the years that followed, the English-speaking world was swept by wave after wave of panics involving satanists, strange illnesses and aliens. In most cases, whatever the substance of the rumour, the people spreading it adopted a similarly casual approach to gathering evidence: anecdotes were treated as data. This approach suited, and was partly dictated by, the requirements of the media. For a hard-pressed news editor, anguished testimony trumps dry and possibly inconclusive statistics every time.

It was not until 1997 that a leading commentator, the feminist scholar Elaine Showalter, was brave enough to join up the dots, as it were, between the angry but empirically dubious claims being made by 'victims' of apparently unrelated syndromes. In that year she published a controversial book, *Hystories*, which lumped together what she called 'hysterical epidemics'. In addition to satanic ritual abuse, it singled out alien abduction, chronic fatigue syndrome (CFS, known as ME in Britain), recovered memory, Gulf War syndrome and multiple personality disorder.[33] Showalter's argument was that the pressure of modern life, coupled with the demands of an insatiable media, was turning 'microtales of individual affliction' into widespread panic about imaginary evils – networks of devil-worshippers, a mysterious 'fatigue virus', invading aliens and a bogus psychological disorder.

After the book came out, Showalter received death threats. Pressure groups were furious that she had labelled them as fantasists. They were even more enraged by the company in which she placed them. 'Boy, does this make my blood boil!' wrote Terri Dorothy, a chronic fatigue sufferer, on a Google discussion group. 'How could she possibly compare someone suffering from CFS with little grey aliens?'[34] But that was what was so audacious about *Hystories* – its readiness to bracket 'respectable' and (in sociological terms) 'deviant' ideas. Of course, the notion of CFS as a single infectious disease, as opposed to a bundle of ailments mostly of psychological origin, is not as absurd as the proposition that aliens are carrying out Mengele-style medical experiments in the middle of the night. But it might well be equally – that is, totally – untrue.

The hysterical epidemics of the 1990s were the first example of assorted cultic ideas simultaneously grabbing hold of the public imagination – with terrible consequences for parents accused of satanism or child abuse merely on the basis of 'recovered' memories. 'Believe the children!' people said; or 'Are you calling me a liar?' Victims, lobby groups and journalists behaved as if all that was required to validate an implausible claim was a sufficiently compelling personal narrative. To quote one of the slogans of that citadel of counterknowledge, the Church of Scientology: 'If it's true for you, it's true.'

Such an approach plays down the value of objective knowledge, and it is significant that the spread of bogus information in the 1980s and 1990s coincided with postmodernist claims, first advanced by the French philosopher Jean-François Lyotard, that orthodox science was essentially a language game played by a white male elite. This world view found powerful reinforcement in the phenomenon of political correctness, in which the boundaries of knowledge are gerrymandered around people's sensitivities.

I will never forget the experience of attending a seminar at Boston University in 1999 at which a group of academics and a couple of rap artists discussed the penetration of the black community by conspiracy theories. In particular, they talked about the rumour that the US government had developed AIDS as a weapon against black Americans. I noticed that no one was making the obvious point that the rumour was baseless, so during the question-and-answer session I asked each of the panellists whether he or she personally believed that AIDS had been cooked up in a government laboratory. Nobody said they did. Equally, nobody said they didn't. One of the speakers, Professor Glenn Loury, currently director of the Institute on Race and Social Division at Boston University, explained that he didn't want to be 'disrespectful' to his own African-American community by giving his real opinion.

The left has helped to spread counterknowledge by insisting on the rights of ethnic, sexual and religious minorities to believe falsehoods that make them feel better about themselves. In 2007, for example, a report by the Department for Education and Skills revealed that some British schoolteachers are dropping the Nazi Holocaust from lessons rather than confront the Holocaust-denial views of Muslim pupils.[35] Another example, which we shall discuss later, is the teaching of Afrocentric history, which relies on pseudoscholarship to argue that the origins of Western civilization lie in black Africa.

But left-wing multiculturalists are not the only guilty ones; entrepreneurs are busy turning counterknowledge into an industry. Publishing houses pay self-taught archaeologists and pseudo-historians a lot of money to turn fragments of fact into saleable stories. Titles are placed in the history sections of bookshops the claims of which have been thoroughly demolished by scholars; yet the publishers pay no attention and carry on bringing out new editions. The dividing line between fiction and non-fiction is becoming increasingly hard to draw. These days, public opinion is so malleable that a product does not even have to pretend to be fact in order to affect perceptions of truth: the success of Dan Brown's thriller *The Da Vinci Code* has persuaded 40 per cent of Americans that the churches are concealing information about Jesus.[36]

Meanwhile, publishers, television channels and newspapers are making huge profits from another branch of counterknowledge: alternative medicine. Unqualified nutritionists make claims for vitamin supplements and 'superfoods' that are unsupported by the scientific literature on the subject; conveniently, the nutritionists often have a commercial interest in selling the supplements in question. Fashionable advocates of alternative medicine, and the executives who commission best-selling books and television series from them, are as reliant on counterknowledge as any schizophrenic bedsit conspiracy theorist. The miracle ('cancer-preventing') diets and the health scares they promote help to undermine science by distorting the public understanding of cause and effect, and therefore of risk.

The fingerprints of the alternative medicine lobby are all over the worst British health scare of recent years, in which thousands of parents denied their children the perfectly safe MMR triple vaccine against measles, mumps and rubella, following the dissemination of flawed data linking it to autism. In that case, distrust of orthodox medicine increased the danger of a measles epidemic.

But that is nothing compared to the consequences of medical counterknowledge in underdeveloped countries. In northern Nigeria, Islamic leaders have issued a fatwa declaring the polio vaccine to be an American conspiracy to sterilize Muslims. Polio has returned to the area, and pilgrims have carried it to Mecca and Yemen. In January

2007, the parents of 24,000 children in Pakistan refused to allow health workers to vaccinate their children because radical mullahs had told them the same idiotic story.[37]

These incidents cannot be dismissed as examples of medieval superstition; northern Nigerians and Pakistanis do not reject life-saving vaccines because they reject modern medicine, but because their leaders are spouting Islamized versions of Western conspiracy theories. Counterknowledge, with its ingrained hostility towards a political, intellectual and scientific elite, appeals to anti-American, anti-Western sentiment in the developing world. Islamic countries, in particular, have embraced counterknowledge to a remarkable degree. In 2006, the Pew Research Center asked Muslims in Indonesia, Egypt, Turkey, Jordan and Pakistan whether Arabs carried out the 9/11 attacks. The majority of respondents in every single country said no. Indeed, most British Muslims – 56 per cent – also thought that Arabs were innocent.[38] A more recent survey, by Channel 4 News, reveals that a quarter of British Muslims believe that 'the British government was involved in some way' with the London terrorist bombings of 7 July 2005.[39] Perhaps even more worryingly, a 2006 National Opinion Poll survey for Channel 4's *Dispatches* found that only 29 per cent of British Muslims believed that the Holocaust happened 'as history teaches it'. Of the rest, 17 per cent said it had been exaggerated, 23 per cent had not heard of it, 24 per cent had no opinion, 6 per cent said they didn't know, and 2 per cent said it never happened.[40]

The reason I single out Muslims in this way is that the conjunction of radical Islam and counterknowledge is particularly dangerous. I don't mean to suggest that Islam's foundational doctrines are especially susceptible to empirically dubious propositions (though I do believe that the absence of an Islamic Enlightenment makes it hugely more vulnerable to pseudoscience). All major religions make claims about the material world, either now or in the past, that non-members believe are patently false. However implausible the theory that Americans masterminded the attacks on the Twin Towers, it does not strain credulity nearly so much as a Palestinian carpenter coming back to life after his execution, or the parting of the Red Sea, or Muhammad's night journey to Jerusalem. In all of these stories, the laws of nature are suspended. Aren't they counterknowledge, along with every superstition and magical belief?

The answer is that religion (which as a concept is notoriously hard to define) shades into counterknowledge, but is not merely a particular variety of it. If you believe that the Holy Spirit exists, no one can prove you wrong. That is not counterknowledge. If you claim that the Holy Spirit cured you of cancer, then that also is untestable: no one can demonstrate that God was not working through the natural or medical processes that led to your cure. If you claim that the Holy Spirit has given you the power to cure other people's cancer without recourse to medicine, then that claim can be tested and found to be wrong. This does not make you a liar; it does mean that you have disseminated a dangerous form of counterknowledge.

Religion becomes proper counterknowledge only when it seriously seeks to undermine, or is contradicted by, the evidence of our senses. There is no reason to believe that the historical miracles claimed by any faith actually happened; but common sense tells us that there is a practical difference between declaring one's belief in isolated supernatural events such as the Resurrection, which is what ordinary churchgoers do, and making falsifiable statements about the world around us, which is what faith healers do.

This is not to let organized religion off the hook. On the contrary, when it does throw its weight behind counterknowledge, the results can be horribly toxic. For example, in 2003 the BBC reported that Cardinal Alfonso López Trujillo, one of the Vatican's most senior cardinals, was spreading the message that the AIDS virus can pass easily through latex condoms.[41] This is a scientific claim that conveniently bolsters Catholic teaching on the immorality of using condoms. It is also false, and lethal: an invitation to HIV-positive men and women to have unprotected sex with their partners. In September 2007 the leader of the Catholic Church in Mozambique, Archbishop Francisco

Chimoio of Maputo, told the BBC that European-made condoms were deliberately infected with HIV, and that some antiretroviral drugs were also infected 'in order to finish off the African people'.[42]

One of the most worrying – not to say stupid and unnecessary – trends in the twenty-first century is the embrace of modern pseudoscience and pseudohistory by representatives of major religions. As we shall see in the following chapter, Christian and Muslim entrepreneurs are investing heavily in a parody of science that is becoming ever more slickly packaged and sophisticated: Creationism, at the click of a mouse.

2

Creationism and Counterknowledge

An American children's website called Kids 4 Truth features a beautiful animated sequence in which scraps of metal fall from the sky. These scraps then mysteriously turn themselves into cogs and dials that slot together *by chance* into a fully functioning pocket watch.[1] As this happens, the narrator reads a little verse:

> 'Ridiculous story!'
> You say with a grin.
> 'Impossible, laughable,
> Surely a sin!'

This is a Creationist website. The animation is based on the 'watchmaker' analogy devised by the eighteenth-century English philosopher William Paley. If you found a watch by the side of the road, he said, its complexity would tell you that someone had designed it. The universe is infinitely more complicated than a watch, ergo it was designed. Modern philosophers and theologians regard Paley's argument as hopelessly naive, but Creationists still accept it. By showing the watch spookily assembling itself by accident, Kids 4 Truth are mocking the Darwinian argument that nature works without divine intervention. They do indeed believe that the theory of evolution is 'surely a sin'.

The next thing we see is an animated biological cell, depicted in all its complexity. The verse continues:

> Now the doctors from Oxford
> Say cells came by chance
> From Goo down to You
> In a beautiful dance.
> What's wrong with their thinking
> To have such odd notions,
> That cells could just happen
> From dirt and warm oceans?

The analogy between Paley's watch and a cell is significant. It shows that Kids 4 Truth are familiar with the most sophisticated and up-to-date argument for Creationism: Intelligent Design.

This term, often referred to simply as ID, entered the scientific vocabulary in about 1990. Initially, it was employed by the authors of Creationist textbooks as an alternative to 'Creation science', the teaching of which in state schools was declared unconstitutional by a Supreme Court ruling in 1987 on the grounds that it breached the separation of church and state.[2] But it soon took on a life of its own, developing into an ingenious series of refutations of the theory of evolution through natural selection – so ingenious, in fact, that some commentators thought Charles Darwin's ideas would soon be written off as just another Victorian eccentricity.

Nearly two decades later, Intelligent Design is still winning educated converts. Even its opponents concede that it cannot be dismissed as the propaganda of semi-educated Christian fundamentalists. Its best-known exponent, Michael Behe, is professor of biochemical sciences at Lehigh University, Pennsylvania. Another leading advocate is William Dembski, a brilliant American mathematician. Lots of supporters of ID are not Christians at all.

In 1996, Behe published a best-selling book called *Darwin's Black Box: The Biochemical Challenge to Evolution*, based around the proposition that 'systems of horrendous, irreducible complexity inhabit a cell'.[3] That sounds uncontroversial, but it isn't. The key word here is 'irreducible', which is intended to bring the whole edifice of Darwinian theory crashing down.

An irreducibly complex system is one that cannot work if even one of its components is removed or slightly altered. Only when all the components are in place and working properly does the system work; therefore *it cannot have evolved*, because it is functionally useless until the last piece of the jigsaw is in place.

Behe uses the analogy of a mousetrap, which might seem like a simple device but is actually irreducibly complex in the sense that it works only when everything is in place. Imagine an alternative reality in which mouse-control devices could evolve through random mutation. There would be no reason for a half-evolved mousetrap to develop into a three-quarters-evolved mousetrap, because the latter would be as useless as the former. The fact that the trap catches mice must mean that it was designed with its function in mind.[4] And what is true of mousetraps is also true of other 'irreducibly complex' systems, such as the human immune system or even the single cell. Behe's conclusion: life itself was designed by an intelligent agent.

All of which sounds plausible enough to the layman. But not a single world-class scientist in the fields of evolutionary biology, physics or geology is persuaded by the mousetrap analogy (we shall see why later). Not one has endorsed Intelligent Design. In September 2005, thirty-eight Nobel laureates wrote to the Kansas State Board of Education begging it not to allow ID to be taught in science classes. The signatories included the vast majority of the winners of the Nobel Prizes for physics, chemistry and medicine over the previous five years.[5]

The US National Academy of Sciences has said that

'Intelligent Design and other claims of supernatural intervention in the origin of life' are not science because they cannot be tested by experiment, do not generate any predictions, and propose no new hypotheses of their own.[6] And in December 2005, US district judge John E. Jones ruled that the Dover area school board in Pennsylvania – the first in the country to insert ID into a science curriculum – had clearly violated the constitutional separation of church and state. Jones, a churchgoing Republican, described ID as 'a religious view, a mere relabelling of Creationism and not a scientific theory'. [7]

Intelligent Design is an important example of counterknowledge, not only because it masquerades so confidently as knowledge, but also because we can trace its evolution from much more primitive forms of belief. ID grew out of 'scientific Creationism' (in which bogus archaeology and bogus geology try to demonstrate the literal truth of Genesis), which in turn grew out of old-fashioned Biblebashing Creationism. But, far from becoming extinct, those primitive forms are interbreeding with ID to produce new varieties of Creationism that combine religious fundamentalism and pseudoscience.

But hang on, you might say: how can I be confident that ID is counterknowledge when many of Behe's arguments – which involve the locking together of amino acids and nucleotides and the intricacies of biosynthetic pathways – are too technical for me to follow? My answer is that I am doing something deeply unfashionable: I am taking the word of scientists on trust.

There are good reasons to trust scientists whenever a huge majority of them endorse an empirical claim. The tests applied to empirical statements are, for the most part, impressively rigorous, and they are applied by a scientific community that (unlike that of Creationists) is made up of individuals from diverse ethnic, religious and cultural backgrounds. Advances in technology and methodology have greatly increased our ability to iden-tify regularities in nature through repeated observation – the essence of scientific endeavour.[8] Of course, from time to time scientists arrive at the wrong explanation of natural phenomena; but these mistakes are usually rectified by later hypotheses that better fit the data. So, when scrupulous researchers overwhelmingly agree that a particular claim is a statement of fact, the probability that they are right is extremely high.

Does that sound naive? It shouldn't. Nothing could be more reasonable than insisting that people measure the evidence of their senses in the most painstaking and nit-picking ways they can devise.

When scientists disagree with each other, that trust inevitably starts to evaporate. If the scientific community is seriously divided on a subject and we want to form an opinion, we must do at least some of the hard work of sifting evidence for ourselves. But, to pick an example at random, we don't need to choose whether to believe that plants make sugar from sunlight through photosynthesis; scientists know how this extremely complicated biochemical process works, and the rest of us happily absorb a simplified explanation of it in the classroom. There may be a maverick scientist somewhere who thinks plants absorb most of their energy from moonlight, but we can safely ignore his thesis because scientists have already sifted through a mass of contradictory evidence.

Let us return to the subject of evolution. The idea that all complex life forms developed from simpler life forms, and that all organisms are in some way related, is only a 'theory' in the sense that no empirical proposition can ever be 100 per cent proven. In the words of John Dupré, professor of philosophy of science at Exeter University, the core propositions of the theory of evolution 'are as unquestionably true as anything that science has established'.[9] As true as photosynthesis, if you like.

Dupré divides the converging evidence supporting evolution (also called 'descent with modification') into three areas. First, there is the physiological evidence of related structures. The forelimbs of all mammals – the bat's wing, the whale's flipper, the human arm – share exactly the same arrangement of bones, even though they serve different purposes. Also, all organisms share the same relations between DNA sequences and the structure of amino acids. 'The overwhelmingly compelling explanation of this and countless parallel examples is descent from common ancestors,' says Dupré. Second, there is the evidence of fossils, whose pattern of descent is wholly consistent with the pattern of relationship suggested by physiological comparisons. Third, there is biogeography, the distribution of different species in which patterns of evolution match patterns of migration, as Darwin discovered after studying finches in the Galapagos Islands.[10]

Moreover, evolution *can* explain so-called irreducible complexity. Behe's ingenious mousetrap analogy falls apart on closer examination. Robert Ehrlich, professor of physics at George Mason University, Virginia, has shown how, theoretically, mouse-control devices could evolve into a mousetrap. His explanation is complicated – but then so is evolution. Essentially, it involves different parts of the device changing shape for different reasons. At various points these mutations would act, singly or together, to change the property of the whole device. Eventually, it might – *might* – evolve into a mousetrap as a result of an enormous number of mutations, none of which has any particular 'goal'.[11]

So natural evolution is a fact. We can safely describe it as such because the probability that it is untrue is so small. Scientists disagree about the respective importance of selection and random mutation, and there is a separate dispute about the meaning of gaps in the fossil record. The late Stephen Jay Gould proposed that these gaps reflected sudden bursts of evolution; other scientists maintain that the gaps were caused by the way the rocks were formed. Morcover, there have also been some vicious disputes about the social implications of evolution – vicious enough for Andrew Brown to entitle his book on the controversy *The Darwin Wars*.[12]

These 'Darwin wars' are, however, fought between scientists who accept descent through modification as true. The battle between evolution and Intelligent Design belongs to another war altogether: one between science and religiously inspired pseudoscience.

Intelligent Design is not science because, as the US National Academy of Sciences points out, its propositions are not falsifiable: there is no way to test them. It is not quite theology either, but it is predicated on belief in some sort of deity. Although Behe and his colleagues deliberately say nothing about the identity of the creator of life and how or why he/she/it went about the project, ID has been embraced almost exclusively by Christians, Muslims and other monotheists. The movement likes to think of its critics as atheist scientists whose intellects are too narrow to contemplate the possibility that the universe was designed for a purpose.

Some biologists, such as Richard Dawkins, are indeed proselytizing atheists. But many others are Christians who argue that, since evolutionary theory cannot explain the original act of Creation, there is no objection to believing that God created matter and then worked through natural evolution. Also, most Christian theologians and clergy agree with them. 'Theistic evolution' is the default position of mainstream Christianity. The proportion of members of the Church of England's General Synod who accept evolution is almost certainly much higher than that in the English population at large.

What about the Roman Catholic Church? The story of the Vatican's flirtation with Intelligent Design is very revealing. Even in the late nineteenth century, the Catholic Church was less uniformly hostile than conservative Protestantism towards the theory of evolution. In 1909, the Pontifical Biblical Commission issued a decree that allowed Catholics to interpret the 'days' in the Book of Genesis as representing indefinite periods of time. As Don O'Leary, the historian of Catholicism and science, notes: 'This was of major significance when arguing that God worked through secondary causes when creating the heavens and the earth.'[13]

Versions of the theory of evolution were accepted by many Catholic theologians during the twentieth century, but it was not until 1996 that Darwin received qualified papal approval. In that year, Pope John Paul II described evolution as 'no longer a mere hypothesis'. The pope said: 'It is indeed remarkable that this theory [of evolution] has been progressively accepted by researchers, following a series of discoveries in various fields of knowledge. The convergence, neither sought nor fabricated, of the results of work that was conducted independently is in itself a significant argument in favour of this theory.'[14] Michael Behe is himself a Catholic, so one can imagine his horror at this statement.

Under the papacy of Benedict XVI, however, the situation has become confused. In July 2005, Cardinal Christoph Schönborn of Vienna, a close ally of Pope Benedict and a possible future pope, wrote in the *New York Times*: 'Evolution in the sense of common ancestry might be true, but evolution in the neo-Darwinian sense – an unguided, unplanned process of random variation and natural selection – is not. Any system of thought that denies or seeks to explain away the overwhelming evidence for design in biology is ideology, not science.'[16]

Catholic scientists were aghast. Where was this overwhelming evidence? Schönborn appeared to have signed up to Intelligent Design. He had been encouraged and helped to write his essay by Mark Ryland, a senior fellow of the Discovery Institute of Seattle's Center for Science and Culture, the most important organization in the Intelligent Design movement; Behe is another senior fellow. For one of the Catholic Church's most intellectually gifted cardinals to pronounce against the Darwinian consensus was a real triumph.

The outcry from scientists was such that, soon afterwards, Schönborn clarified his remarks. Evolutionary theory was not incompatible with belief in God, he said, so long as scientists do not overstep the boundaries of their discipline and claim that 'everything ... from the Big Bang to Beethoven's Ninth Symphony ... is principally, exclusively and irrevocably seen as a product of chance'.[16]

Schönborn's revised opinion was compatible with theistic evolution; he appeared to have backed away from supporting ID. Even so, the whole business unnerved Catholic scientists who had been delighted by John Paul II's support for the theory of evolution. Matters were further confused in November 2005 when Pope Benedict said in off-the-cuff remarks that Creation was an 'intelligent project' and criticized those who said that it was 'without direction'. These comments were consistent with theistic evolution *and* Intelligent Design, though the consensus among Catholic commentators is that Benedict does not endorse ID. In January 2006, an article appeared in the Vatican newspaper *L'Osservatore Romano* arguing that ID is not science; but the article, although approved by church officials, was not a statement of policy.[17]

The truth is that the Vatican had come within a whisker of endorsing pseudoscience, thus creating precisely the sort of conflict between faith and reason that the modern church has tried to avoid.

Perhaps if Cardinal Schönborn had spent more time studying the antecedents and allies of Intelligent Design he would have thought twice before endorsing it. Like so many varieties of counterknowledge, ID forms part of a whole ecosystem in which information from the cultic milieu mutates into a form that can survive in the mainstream. Or, to use another metaphor, ID is the Trojan horse of renascent Creationism.

The spokesmen for Intelligent Design tend not to be fundamentalist Christians whose literal reading of Genesis leads them to conclude that the earth is 6,000 years old. But there is no copyright on the concept of Intelligent Design, and 'young-earth' Creationists frequently invoke its arguments.[18]

ID has been appropriated by the Institute for Creation Research, the major organ of young-earth 'scientific Creationism', which teaches that the doctrine of evolution has inspired communism, imperialism, bestiality, infanticide, slavery and child abuse. The Institute's website links Intelligent Design and 'Flood geology', arguing that fossil deposits left by Noah's Flood reveal the 'ordering principle' discovered by Behe et al.[19] And, as we shall see, the Islamic world has also latched on to Intelligent Design.

Creationism in general is flourishing in America, in both its crudest and its most sophisticated varieties. President George W. Bush, while not endorsing Intelligent Design, has suggested, to his shame, that it could be discussed as a scientific theory in state schools. A 2004 Gallup poll found that around 45 per cent of Americans believe that God created human beings in their present form about 10,000 years ago. So about 100 million adult Americans are ignorant of the origins of human life. (Anatomically modern humans are at least 100,000 years old.) But the really shocking thing about this statistic is that the proportion of scientifically illiterate respondents has not changed significantly, and may even have risen, since the question was first asked in 1982.[20]

Why should this be the case, in a country in which the teaching of Creationism in science lessons is unconstitutional because it breaches the separation of church and state? The growth of the religious right is often mentioned as a factor; but there is no evidence that there has been a growth in fundamentalist churches for which hard-line Creationism is a test of theological correctness. Even in conservative Christian universities very few science faculties are prepared to teach young-earth Creationism, or even Intelligent Design.

The continued vigour of Creationism owes more to technology than to traditional religious revivalism. Independent sources create custom-designed material that shoots through cyberspace and the ether, where it is picked up by ordinary people, religious and ethnic minorities, oddballs, cultists, maverick academics and fanatics.

We should not be surprised. In the modern world, counterknowledge is far more likely to be packaged as entertainment or as a user-friendly learning experience than as a stern lecture. Bogus information can even provide a fun day out for all the family, as Alec Russell of the *Daily Telegraph* discovered when he was given a preview of the world's first Creation Museum in Ohio, which opened in 2007.

Russell was shown animatronic children and dinosaurs playing together in the Garden of Eden. His guide, Ken Ham, from the fast-growing young-earth organization Answers in Genesis, explained that dinosaurs survived Noah's Flood and roamed the earth until quite recently. 'There are dragon legends all over the world. Why? Because they have a basis in truth, a basis in real animals. So, even though the word dinosaur wasn't coined until 1841, we would say that it's very possible that what people today call dinosaurs were known as dragons.' But how did they manage to fit such gigantic creatures on to Noah's Ark? 'They only took young dinosaurs on board,' says Ham.

Russell describes the Creation Museum as a place that Americans who reject evolution 'can visit for a jolly family weekend, while having their views reinforced in a series of exhibitions, displays and films which argue that evolutionary science is no more than a fairy tale'.[21] I would go further, and say that audience-targeting attractions such as the museum can turn Christians who are vaguely opposed to evolution into Creationists, just as other forms of 'infotainment' turn natural sceptics into conspiracy theorists.

Technological expertise is crucial; the museum's creative director used to design sets for Universal Studios in Hollywood. The transformation of America into what the cultural critic Neal Gabler calls a 'republic of entertainment', in which the primary purpose of information is to stimulate the senses and the imagination, greatly increases receptivity to counterknowledge. The Creation Museum has borrowed animatronics from *Jurassic Park* to propagate its own fiction; one fiction has inspired another.

New technology is egalitarian; it is good at dismantling hierarchies of knowledge. Anyone with the appropriate expertise can redesign and then market counterknowledge in ways that appeal to an audience that cares more about presentation than content. Creationist websites are more colourful, accessible and numerous than those that explain how evolution works. If you typed 'Creation' into the Google search engine in March 2007, the second of 308 million results, beaten only by a nightclub called Creation, was Kids 4 Truth – Creation, describing itself as 'a multi-media blast'.[22] And that last claim is certainly accurate: the site *is* a blast, a collection of cute, child-friendly Flash 'dynamations'.

As we saw at the beginning of this chapter, Kids 4 Truth makes use of the ID concept of irreducible complexity. But, groovy graphics notwithstanding, it also reflects the views of the most unyielding young-earth Creationists – fundamentalist Protestants who think that even Behe is probably going to Hell because he is a Roman Catholic. Kids 4 Truth believes in a literal 144-hour creation of the world; a more accurate name for the organization might be Kids 4 Untruth. Churches can sign up to the package, buy the Powerpoint presentations and graphic tools and set up Kids 4 Truth clubs, so long as they agree not to deviate from the strict teaching programme, described as a 'catechism on steroids'. But any parents can encourage their children to add the Kids 4 Truth site to their bookmarks.

The organization behind the website is the Servant Christian Community Foundation, a Kansas-based charitable organization that specializes in advising Christians on tax-efficient ways of funding the spread of the Gospel. But there are several different contributors to Kids 4 Truth, and overall it operates more as a coalition of fundamentalist ministries than as a single structure. And this is true of so much internet-driven counterknowledge: individual sites, however carefully policed, are essentially portals on to a world view.

A spectacular illustration of this approach is CreationWiki, a Creationist alternative to the web encyclopedia Wikipedia, which by 2007 had assembled over 2,500 articles written from a young-earth perspective.[23] In March 2007, the main article flagged on the home page was about the eruption at Mount St Helens, Washington, on 18 May 1980, which killed fifty-seven people – the deadliest volcanic event in the history of the United States. According to the article, the Mount St Helens eruption created thick deposits of sedimentary rock that were very rapidly eroded into canyons. Therefore the Grand Canyon, instead of being carved out over millions of years by the Colorado River, as geologists believe, could have been created by an 'event' as recent as Noah's Flood.[24]

The authority for this claim is Dr Steve Austin, chairman of the department of geology at the Institute for Creation Research Graduate School. Some of Austin's analysis of lava flows is far too technical for a layman to evaluate. However, he has been unable to cite a single article in a peer-reviewed journal in support of his Mount St Helens thesis. His critics, on the other hand, have raised innumerable scientific objections to it, one of the most striking of which is that there is a huge difference between the 'sedimentary rock' (actually volcanic ash) deposited by the St Helens eruption and true sedimentary rocks, such as limestone or sandstone, for which there is no evidence of rapid deposition and erosion at the Grand Canyon or anywhere else.

The number of professional geologists who believe that the Mount St Helens eruption provides fresh evidence of Noah's Flood is the same as the number of Nobel Prize winners who believe in Intelligent Design: zero. The Wikipedia and CreationWiki entries for Mount St Helens represent knowledge versus counterknowledge. Yet the layout of the web pages is identical, down to the point size and colour of the font. That is because the software that powers Wikipedia is in the public domain and can be used by anyone to build another encyclopedia.

'Free culture knows no bounds,' says Jimmy Wales, founder of Wikipedia. 'We welcome the reuse of our work to build variants. That's directly in line with our mission.'[25] Wikipedia itself is, by its nature, unreliable; a fair amount of counterknowledge creeps into its database every day. But, so long as its users are aware of its serious limitations, it is a useful resource. The purpose of CreationWiki and another anti-evolution rival, Conservapedia, is to dress up nonsense as science.

Wales is right in one respect: the 'free culture' of the internet does not recognize the bounds between information and misinformation, and it is also increasing the permeability of different bodies of counterknowledge. Once again, Creationism is a good example of this process. The anonymity of cyberspace allows the largest body of Creationists in the world, Muslims, to absorb useful ideas from Christian opponents of evolution.

Muslims are not young-earthers, since the idea that the world is 6,000 years old is extracted from genealogies in the Old Testament and is therefore explicitly Judaeo-Christian. So Islamic Creationists cannot use overtly Christian material from the Institute for Creation Research (though they happily plunder that material for ideas). The argument for Intelligent Design, on the other hand, can easily be adapted by Muslims because it restricts its theology to the notion of a divine designer, who could just as easily be Allah as the Trinitarian God of the Christians. 'Intelligent Design is not alien to Islam,' writes the Turkish political scientist Mustafa Akyol. 'It is very much our cause and we should do everything we can to support it.'

Islamonline.net is a widely read Islamic website run by the Egyptian cleric Yusuf al-Qaradawi, a 'moderate' Muslim who strongly supports Palestinian suicide bombings.[26] The site has issued a 'Call for Action' to Muslims, written by Akyol, asking them to spread the message of Intelligent Design. It tells students: 'Go and learn about Intelligent Design. Learn why Darwinism is wrong. Then raise this issue in your classrooms. Question your biology teachers and your textbooks. Form Muslim Student Associations and get in touch with the Intelligent Design groups in your area. Organize lectures by ID scientists and write under the title "The Fall of Darwinism: The Greatest Myth Ever".' Muslim parents are told: 'If you have children in schools, pay attention to their biology classes. Are they being indoctrinated by the myths of Darwinism? If so, appeal to their school board and question this theory by appealing to the world of the ID scientists. Get help from Christian families who support the Intelligent Design cause.'[27]

Islamic Creationism is turning into a serious problem

for British sixth-form colleges and universities – not just because Creationism is incompatible with biological science, but also because educational establishments are anxious not to offend ethnic-minority pupils and parents.

According to a February 2006 report in the *Guardian*, at one (unnamed) sixth-form college in London 'most biology students are thought to be Creationists'.[28] The report, in a left-leaning newspaper that is traditionally much quicker to criticize evangelical Christians than Muslims, implied rather than stated that the students were Muslim. But anyone familiar with education in London knows that Pakistani Muslim students taking biology A-levels en route to becoming doctors, dentists or scientists vastly outnumber fundamentalist Christians with the same ambition. A biology teacher at the college was quoted as saying: 'The vast majority of my students now believe in Creationism, and these are thinking young people who are able and articulate and not at the dim end at all.'

A 2006 poll of UK higher education students showed that less than 10 per cent of Muslims accepted the theory of evolution.[29] This survey was also reported by the *Guardian*, although the way the findings were presented glossed over the implication that students who identified themselves as Muslims were far more anti-evolution than those who identified themselves as Christians. The newspaper quoted Roger Downie, professor of zoology at Glasgow University, who was alarmed by the number of his own students who were Creationists, and blamed schools for not teaching science properly: 'The impression people get is that science is about accumulating a lot of facts in your head rather than testing of evidence and fine-tuning what you find.'

Steve Jones, professor of genetics at University College London, has spent twenty years visiting schools to talk about evolutionary biology. For the first ten years, only about one student in 1,000 expressed Creationist beliefs. 'Now, in any school I go to, I meet a student who says they are a Creationist or delude themselves that they are,' he says.[30]

In 2006, Muslim medical students at Guy's Hospital in London distributed leaflets attacking Darwinism as part of the Islam Awareness Week. Professors of medicine and biology are expressing deep concern that people who are soon to be doctors reject so many of the fundamental discoveries of biological science. Typically, however, these expressions of concern are either unattributable (because they might open the speaker to the charge of Islamophobia) or balanced by attacks on the soft target of American fundamentalism. Jones describes British Creationism as 'an insidious and growing problem . . . Irrationality is a very infectious disease, as we see from the United States.'

That dig at America is misleading; Muslim Creationism is a far more efficient carrier of irrationality than American Christian fundamentalism. It is true that in Muslim countries there are no theme parks showing baby dinosaurs romping with children; but nor is there a Supreme Court that forbids the teaching of religious belief in science lessons. Yes, it is a scandal that the proportion of the American public that rejects evolution has not fallen in the last twenty years; and it is true that the millions of Americans who regard Darwinism as a conspiracy are also susceptible to other ignorant conspiracy theories. But the Institute for Creation Research is still essentially located in the American cultic milieu; although it makes use of the arguments of the Intelligent Design movement, the latter is careful not to endorse the ICR's absurd young-earth beliefs. Islamic Creationism, by contrast, is a unified and increasingly influential component of a wider Islamic world view that embraces and propagates counterknowledge.

One reason why the new Islamic Creationism is unified is that, to a remarkable degree, it is the product of one man (or possibly several people posing as one man). He writes as Harun Yahya, but his real name, according to his own website, is Adnan Oktar. This self-styled 'prominent Turkish intellectual' was born in 1956, studied at Mimar Sinan University, and boasts that he is 'even more expert' in Western materialist philosophy than its advocates. In recent years, he says, his 'dedicated effort against Darwinism has grown to be a worldwide phenomenon'.[31]

Yahya's documentaries are shown by independent or government-run television channels in Indonesia, Malaysia,

Pakistan, Nigeria, Tanzania, the United Arab Emirates, Azerbaijan and Bosnia, and by satellite to Muslims in Australia, Germany, the Netherlands and the United States. His material has been translated into fifty-one languages. In my local Islamic bookshop in west London, all the books on Creationism – indeed, nearly all the books on biological science – are by Yahya and are produced by one of the publishing houses owned by his Foundation for Scientific Research, the Turkish acronym of which is BAV.

Although Yahya rejects the term 'Intelligent Design' as un-Islamic, his more sophisticated writings, such as *The Miracle of Hormones* (2004),[32] are heavily influenced by the ID notion of irreducible complexity. The BAV also produces an impressively glossy 800-page *Atlas of Creation*, which has been distributed, unsolicited, to schools and colleges around the world; in early 2007 the French education ministry warned schools against the book after several thousand copies arrived in the country, apparently directed at France's large Muslim minority.[33] The atlas tries to deny evolution by showing that today's animals look exactly like their fossilized ancestors, and also says that Darwinism was the inspiration behind the Third Reich and modern terrorism. This is a familiar theme of Yahya's, and brings us to what we might term his less sophisticated writings.

For Yahya, Darwinism is one of the most evil teachings of the 'dark clan', which he describes as 'a web-like structure with offshoots in every country, orchestrating the moral degeneration of today's world'.[34] Freemasons, Nazis, Zionists, drug barons, homosexuals, Buddhists, prostitutes, evolutionary biologists – all are caught up in a global conspiracy whose motto is Darwin's 'survival of the fittest'. (There are unmistakable echoes here of the fundamentalist Christian conspiracy theories of the Institute for Creation Research, which also associates Darwinism with crime and sexual perversion.)

Very few stretches of the cultic milieu are out of bounds to Yahya, as a visit to his website confirms. Harunyahya.com, in addition to offering free downloads of all the author's books, links to forty-two websites based on his work. A site exposing the 'lie' of the Stone Age (thestoneage.org) explains that primitive man never existed: 'For example, Prophet Noah (*pbuh*) knew boat-building technology, for we know from the Qur'an that his ark was steam-powered.' Another of Yahya's sites, Globalfreemasonry.com, borrows wholesale the fanciful theory of British 'historians' Christopher Knight and Robert Lomas that the secrets of Freemasonry can be traced back to ancient Egypt via the Knights Templar.[35] Yahya also cites the 'famous British historian' Nesta Webster (1876–1960), a paranoid anti-Semite who was partly responsible for introducing the British public to the Protocols of the Elders of Zion.[36] Meanwhile, truthforkids.com, aimed at children, is the Islamic equivalent of the Christian fundamentalist Kids 4 Truth.

Just as traditional counterknowledge mimics the structure and style of genuine knowledge rather than its content, newer digital entrepreneurs raid cyberspace for recognizable designs. CreationWiki models itself on Wikipedia. Yahya and the BAV borrow heavily from Western websites: their online bookshop looks like Amazon.com. Cloning a 'respectable' website is far easier than producing a book that looks as if it emanates from a major publisher.

As it happens, Islamic Creationists have enough resources to do both. No one is quite sure why this movement should have sprung up in Turkey, officially a secular state, and no one has publicly identified the source of the BAV's very substantial funds. The BAV has organized Creationist conferences in over 100 Turkish cities and towns; by 2006 it had opened more than eighty 'museums' of Creationism in restaurants, shopping malls and city halls across the country, featuring portraits of Charles Darwin framed in dripping blood.[37]

According to a Reuters report in 2006, Turkish Creationism 'has an influence US Creationists could only dream of'. Pious Muslims in the government have managed to cut back the time allotted for the discussion of evolution in biology classes, reducing it to the status of a contested nineteenth-century theory; in a survey of public acceptance of evolution in thirty-four countries, Turkey, which is pushing hard to join the European Union, came last.[38] 'Darwinism is dying in Turkey thanks to us,' says BAV's director, Tarkan Yavas. 'Darwinism breeds immorality, and an immoral Turkey is of no use to the European Union.'[39] In August 2007, Harun Yahya, a.k.a. Adnan Oktar, succeeded in persuading the Turkish courts to block access to WordPress.com, home of the world's leading blogging software, because it was being used by critics of Creationism who had allegedly libelled him. In other words, the whole of Turkey was prevented from accessing the site and every blog hosted by it.[40]

The situation in the rest of the Islamic world is just as depressing. Creationism has not so far been an important issue in Arab countries because the teaching of science is so perfunctory that Darwin's theories have scarcely registered. But, in their attempts to interest Muslims in 'Creation science' via the internet, Yahya and Akyol are pushing at an open door.

In Indonesia, Pakistan and Egypt, the proportion of the population that believes in Darwin's theory of evolution is 2, 5 and 3 per cent, respectively; only in secular Kazakhstan does the figure rise as high as 10 per cent.[41] Meanwhile, as the *Economist* reported in April 2007, Creationism is gaining ground in non-Muslim parts of Africa and the former Soviet Union. In Kenya, evangelical Christians are bitterly opposing plans to put on display Turkana Boy, the most complete skeleton of *Homo erectus* ever found, because they do not believe that *Homo erectus* existed. In Russia, the Moscow patriarchate of the Orthodox

Church has attacked Darwin and supported the teaching of alternatives to evolution in schools.[42] Even the Indian New Age guru Deepak Chopra has revealed himself to be an Intelligent Design Creationist. Writing in the *Huffington Post* in 2005, he sought to elevate the debate over evolution to a 'higher plane' by listing various problems that biologists have failed to address. For example: 'Why are life forms beautiful? Non-beautiful creatures have survived for millions of years, so have beautiful ones. The notion that this is random seems weak.' What the myopic biological scientists are failing to grasp, adds Chopra, is that the universe itself knows what it is doing. 'Consciousness may exist in photons, which seem to be the carrier of all information in the universe.'[43]

Chopra, who has a significant following among middle-class Indians, is anxious to distance himself from Christian Creationism, which he associates with religious and political fanaticism. But his own 'objections' to evolution are no more sophisticated than those of fundamentalist Christians or Muslims, and they are equally invalid.

Creationism in all its forms does incalculable damage; no other form of pseudoscience undermines so many scientific discoveries. If you refuse to acknowledge the awesome explanatory power of the theory of evolution, you can never properly understand astronomy, anthropology, biology, geology, palaeontology, physics or zoology. The social, political and cultural implications of such ignorance are profoundly disturbing. A society that does not breed specialists in most or all of these fields cannot expect to evolve into a competitive economy. In rejecting 'Darwinism', the developing world thinks it is demonstrating moral superiority over degenerate Western values. In fact, it is doing nothing of the sort. It is rejecting the scientific method itself, and thereby condemning future generations to material and intellectual poverty.

3

The Return of Pseudohistory

Has anyone revealed that after Jesus married the notorious Freemason, Mary Magdalene, in a ceremony on top of the Great Pyramid of Giza, she spirited him off to the south of France in one of the FBI's black helicopters?

If not, it can only be a matter of time. We are living in a golden age of bogus history and archaeology, some of which is easily identifiable as rubbish and some of which is pseudoscholarship carefully dressed up to look authentic. The easiest place to discover historical counterknowledge is the internet – failing that, any major bookshop in Britain or North America.

Until a few years ago, nearly all the bogus history could be found on shelves marked 'Mysteries', 'Esoteric' or 'Occult'. Now you can find pseudohistory in the history section. As I write, Britain's two biggest chains of bookstores, Waterstone's and Borders/Books *etc.*, are selling a volume called *1421: The Year China Discovered the World* as 'recommended history'. This book is not history at all;

as we shall see, it is a work of the most devious bogus scholarship. An even more disturbing development is that a certain type of pseudohistory, material that has crossed the border from bias into pure invention, is being taught in schools and universities and targeted at an ethnic minority – but more of that later.

The public has been buying works of speculative archaeology and history in increasing numbers for many years. Oddly, however, it was a work of fiction, Dan Brown's thriller *The Da Vinci Code*, which has sold 40 million copies since 2003, that alerted authors, publishers and film-makers to the full commercial potential of historical counter-knowledge. It also had an effect on people's understanding of Christian history. As we saw in chapter one, a large proportion of the American public is now receptive to conspiracy theories involving Jesus: 40 per cent think that the churches are concealing information about him.[1]

The publication of *The Da Vinci Code* was an important event in the annals of pseudohistory. The book was a novel, yet at its heart lay a controversial historical narrative (in itself, perfectly legitimate territory for fiction) which Brown insisted was not fiction but proven historical fact. Indeed, he begins the story with a page marked 'Fact', which says: 'The Priory of Sion – a European Secret Society founded in 1099 – is a real organization. In 1975 Paris's Bibliothèque Nationale discovered parchments known as Les Dossiers Secrets, identifying numerous members of the Priory of

Sion, including Sir Isaac Newton, Sandro Botticelli, Victor Hugo and Leonardo da Vinci.'[2]

In the course of the novel, we learn that Jesus married Mary Magdalene, who bore him a child; their descendants became the Merovingian kings of France. The secret of the Messianic bloodline is protected by the Priory of Sion, which celebrates the principle of the 'divine feminine' that lies at the heart of true Christianity. According to Brown, Leonardo da Vinci hinted at the truth in his *Last Supper*, in which the androgynous St John is actually the Magdalene. The Roman Catholic Church also knows this secret, and is desperate to suppress the truth. Again, this is a conspiracy theory to which Dan Brown actually subscribes.

The theory is not new. In 1982, Michael Baigent, Richard Leigh and Henry Lincoln published *The Holy Blood and the Holy Grail*, which introduced English-speaking readers to the connection between the Magdalene, the Merovingians and the Priory of Sion. They themselves partly based their work on a book called *Le Trésor maudit de Rennes-le-Château* (1967) by Gérard de Sède, a self-confessed hoaxer and forger of historic documents. *Holy Blood, Holy Grail*, as it was called in America, became an instant best-seller. The extraction of code words from Les Dossiers Secrets impressed readers; so did the apparent discovery of geometric patterns in a Poussin painting that formed part of the mystery. In short, the book was one of the first works of 'alternative' history for many years to persuade a sceptical audience that, despite its more fanciful passages, there 'might be something in' its claims.

In reality, however, *The Holy Blood and the Holy Grail* was pure pseudohistory: more professionally produced than its predecessors, but no less intellectually dishonest. Laura Miller, writing for *Salon* in 2004, described Baigent, Leigh and Lincoln as 'the Moriartys of pseudohistory . . . their techniques include burying their readers in chin-high drifts of factoids – some valid but irrelevant, some uncheckable (the untranslated diaries of obscure 17th-century clerics, and so on), others, like the labyrinthine family trees of various medieval French noblemen, simply numbing, and if you trouble to figure them out, pretty inconclusive'.

A preposterous idea will first be floated as a guess (it is 'not inconceivable' that the Knights Templar found documentation of Jesus and Mary Magdalene's marriage in Jerusalem), then later presented as a tentative hypothesis, then still later treated as a fact . . . Each detail requires extensive effort to track down and verify, but anyone who succeeds in proving it false comes across as a mere nitpicker – and still has a blizzard of other pseudofacts to contend with. The miasma of bogus authenticity that the authors of *Holy Blood, Holy Grail* create becomes impenetrable; you might as well use a rifle to fight off a thick fog.[3]

Ken Mondschein, reviewing a 2004 reprint of the book in the *New York Press*, made fun of the notion that the bloodline of Jesus and Mary Magdalene could have been preserved: 'The idea of keeping the family tree pruned to bonsai-like proportions is also completely fallacious. Infant mortality in pre-modern times was ridiculously high, and you'd only need one childhood accident or disease in 2,000 years to wipe out the bloodline; if, however, even one extra sibling per generation survived to reproduce, the numbers of descendants would increase at an exponential rate; keep the children of Christ marrying each other, on the other hand, and eventually they'd be so inbred that the sons of God would have flippers for feet.' [4]

But we do not need to rely on internal inconsistencies to discredit *The Holy Blood and the Holy Grail*. In the 1990s, Baigent, Leigh and Lincoln learned that they had been the victims of an elaborate hoax. The Priory of Sion, it turned out, was founded as recently as the late 1940s by Pierre Plantard, a fake French aristocrat; the 'medieval' Priory documents were knocked up by Plantard's con-artist friends Philippe de Cherisey and Gérard de Sède in the 1960s, who inserted the code words as a tease.[5]

A BBC2 *Timewatch* documentary exposed the hoax in 1996.[6] Shortly afterwards, I shared a platform with Baigent and Leigh at an Oxford Union seminar about pseudo-history, at which Richard Leigh admitted that he and his fellow authors had been mistaken about the authenticity of Les Dossiers Secrets. 'We were taken in,' he said, looking gratifyingly embarrassed, though he did not provide any more details.

Yet, when *The Da Vinci Code* shot to the top of the best-seller lists, *The Holy Blood and the Holy Grail* was reprinted and placed next to Brown's thriller in bookshops. No mention was made of the hoax. Bizarrely, despite all the money Brown was making for them, Michael Baigent and Richard Leigh sued him for plagiarizing their work. They lost their case and the appeal, and in 2007 found themselves facing a legal bill of £3 million. As Oscar Wilde said of the death of Little Nell, it would have taken a heart of stone not to laugh. Even so, they had already sold 6 million copies of their book. A visitor from Mars (of whom there have been many, according to pseudohistorians) would be confused. How did this peculiar genre develop, and why is it still so popular?

For a loose definition of pseudohistory, it is hard to improve on Wikipedia: 'Pseudohistory is a pejorative term applied to texts which purport to be historical in nature but which depart from standard historiographical conventions in a way which undermines their conclusions.'[7] A watertight definition is impossible because the decision to use the word is always subjective. Even so, there are broadly agreed criteria.

Works can be labelled as pseudohistory for one or more of the following reasons: that the evidence for key facts is speculative, distorted or unsourced; that the work has a political or religious agenda; that competing explanations for the same facts have been ignored; that the work relies on conspiracy theories, when the principle of Occam's razor would recommend a simpler, more prosaic explanation. (The fourteenth-century English Franciscan William of Occam argued that when there are competing explanations of a phenomenon, the one that involves the fewest assumptions and hypotheses is most likely to be true. This 'shaving' of unnecessary assumptions is what gives the principle its name.)

One of the first clashes between real and bogus history took place in the early seventeenth century. In 1590, the Spanish Jesuit scholar José de Acosta, a former missionary in Peru and Mexico, completed *A Natural and Moral History of the Indies*, in which he tackled the question of the origins of the American Indians. The book was widely circulated, and translated into English in 1604. Stephen Williams, former Peabody Professor of American Archaeology at Harvard, describes the book as 'an astounding piece of work . . . which very perceptively dealt with possible alternative hypotheses in a most scientific way'. Working from very limited data, Acosta applied Occam's razor to fashionable theories that the Indians were descendants of Atlanteans or the Lost Tribes of Israel, and dismissed them as fantasy. He concluded that the Indians arrived via a land bridge from Asia – and this was long before the Bering Strait was even known to exist.

Enter Gregorio Garcia, a Dominican priest who had also spent time in the Americas. In 1607 he published *The Origin of the Indians of the New World*, in which he discussed eleven major theories of Indian origin and found evidence to support every single one, including waves of Carthaginian, Atlantean and Israelite immigration. It would not be fair to accuse Garcia of spreading counterknowledge since his opinions reflected the consensus of the time. On the other hand, he has plenty in common with later bogus historians: his work is a methodological mess, which cites many sources but conveniently omits Acosta's work. Williams calls Garcia 'the spiritual father to dozens of equally uncritical mélanges of myths and half-truths about New World cultural origins'.[8]

Indeed, Garcia can be seen as the spiritual father of hyperdiffusionism, the most influential movement in pseudohistory. A hyperdiffusionist theory is one that proposes that the greatest cultural achievements of one ancient civilization can be traced to another, higher civilization whose ideas were transmitted as a result of voyages or other forms of 'diffusion' not recognized by mainstream scholars (usually because they never happened). As a rule of thumb, anyone who tells you that the Egyptians/Minoans/Lost Tribes of Israel built the Mayan pyramids/Easter Island statues/Stonehenge is a hyperdiffusionist. Also, the phrase 'before Columbus', when applied to transatlantic voyages, should set off a warning light, as should the adjective 'lost' when applied to something as intrinsically hard to misplace as a civilization.

The basic world view of the hyperdiffusionist is summed up nicely in a passage from *The Da Vinci Code*. Dan Brown is writing about his hero, Robert Langdon, a 'Harvard professor of religious symbology', who, if he existed in real life, would be lucky to graduate from high school, so fatuous are his theories: 'As someone who had spent his life exploring the hidden interconnectivity of disparate emblems and ideologies, Langdon viewed the world as a web of profoundly intertwined histories and events. *The connections may be invisible*, he often preached to his symbology classes at Harvard, *but they are always there, buried just beneath the surface.*'[9]

This is a medieval way of thinking. Belief in hidden correspondences was almost universal before the Enlightenment, and it went hand in hand with a pre-modern methodology: first you decide what you believe, then you find the evidence, brushing aside anything that doesn't fit. In contrast, the theories of modern scholars are worthless unless they can withstand systematic attempts to disprove them. The emergence of a rigorous post-Enlightenment methodology has banished all sorts of ideas to the cultic milieu. And among the first to be relegated were the tall-tales of the hyperdiffusionists.

'Fantastic archaeology', as Stephen Williams calls it, has been the province of the amateur and the fraudster ever since its golden age in the nineteenth century, when enthusiastic researchers turned the Americas into the Grand Central Station of the ancient world, visited by Greeks, Romans, Celts, Phoenicians, Israelites, Nubians and 'Hindoos'. Admittedly, there is evidence of a short-lived Norse settlement on the far north-eastern tip of North America around the year 1000. But every other scenario is rooted in wishful thinking, error, deceit or a mixture of the three.

Why did people confect these stories? Modern commentators often accuse pseudohistorians of a form of racism: the 'barbarians' of the Central American jungles could not possibly have constructed beautiful cities on an immense scale, so there must have been contact with the truly civilized people of the Old World. European nationalism played its part, too. Accounts of Celts or Norsemen crossing the Atlantic – sometimes, mysteriously, in stone boats – were embraced by their ethnic descendants. In the Midwest, where many Americans were from German and Scandinavian immigrant families, farmers were forever tripping over stones carved with freshly scratched 'Viking runes'.

Today, we think of these nineteenth-century theories as embarrassing historical curiosities, perhaps forgetting that one of the modern world's fastest-growing religions is based on just such a myth. According to the Book of Mormon, the sacred text of the Church of Jesus Christ of

Latter-day Saints, two ancient Near Eastern peoples travelled to the Americas. The first, the 'Jaredites' (identified by some modern Mormons as the Olmecs), reached the New World 2,000 years ago and founded a great civilization, before fighting to extinction. Then in 600 BC Israelites arrived in the Americas and split into Nephites and Lamanites; they were united after a visit from Jesus Christ, but later quarrelled again. The Lamanites wiped out the Nephites and were given a 'skin of blackness' by God to mark their sinfulness; many Mormons believe Lamanites built the Mayan cities and were the ancestors of today's Native Americans.

It goes without saying that the Book of Mormon, supposedly translated from gold plates written in 'Reformed Egyptian' by Joseph Smith in the 1820s, is fiction (and pulverizingly dull fiction at that – Mark Twain described it as 'chloroform in print'). No archaeologist who is not a Mormon believes a word of it. Attempts by Latter-day Saint academics to reconcile their scriptures with recent archaeological findings are comparable in their mock-scholarship to 'Creation science'. Mormonism is the only religion whose major claims have been officially declared to be untrue by the America's National Museum of Natural History, part of the Smithsonian Institution.[10] But then it is the only world religion (13 million members and growing fast) built on a foundation of almost pure counterknowledge.

For most of the twentieth century, however, the more

ambitious the 'alternative' history, the smaller its following. The field became known as 'cult archaeology' because its practitioners behaved as if they themselves had been initiated into a secret society. *The connections may be invisible, but they are always there, buried just beneath the surface*, they told each other. They quarrelled over subjects such as the true location of Atlantis or the hiding place of the Ark of the Covenant, but, in the end, they held fast to their core belief: that there is no such thing as coincidence.

Aren't the ancient monuments of Mexico and the Nile roughly the same triangular shape? Then behold the traces of a single 'master civilization'. Do the myths of Mesopotamia and Scandinavia talk of a great flood? Then they must be describing the same, actual event. Above all, cult archaeologists seized on apparent linguistic similarities between widely scattered peoples. To give just one example: according to Laurence Gardner, author of *Genesis of the Grail Kings* and self-styled Historiographer Royal of the Royal House of Stuart, the migration of Sumerians from Mesopotamia to ancient Ireland is revealed by the Irish word for dragon, *sumaire*.[11]

All of this is easy to mock; but, increasingly, pseudohistorians and cult archaeologists have been able to laugh back at their critics. Nobody would have believed, fifty years ago, that the authors of badly written pseudohistory would routinely sell more than a million copies of their books; that whole sections of bookshops would be given over to speculative archaeology and history; or, worse, that some of this material would be packaged in such a way as to make it difficult to distinguish from scholarship.

Modern cult archaeology first reached a mass market with *Chariots of the Gods?* by the Swiss author Erich von Däniken, which claimed that the monuments of ancient societies – the Egyptian pyramids, Stonehenge, the Easter Island statues – were evidence of prehistoric visitations by space travellers.[12] First published in 1968, it sold over 10 million copies in many languages. No serious scholar took these claims seriously, but von Däniken had demonstrated that there was a potentially enormous market for books that turned ancient history into a series of giant mysteries.

The Holy Blood and The Holy Grail showed how von Däniken's style of reasoning could be applied to religious history and moved slightly upmarket. Baigent, Leigh and Lincoln's pseudohistory is more sophisticated than crude hyperdiffusionism, but its premises are similar. Secret knowledge is passed from one unlikely context to another, and even the knowledge of this transmission is a closely guarded secret. Closely guarded, that is, until Baigent, Leigh and Lincoln, or their rivals, stumble across it. Open a page at random, and there is a good chance you will find a passage that reads: 'We could not believe what we had in our hands. If these documents were what they said they were, then the whole history of [insert as appropriate] would have to be rewritten', etc.

For a few years, it seemed as if myths about secret societies had displaced the ocean-crossing Celts in their stone boats. But then hyperdiffusionism reinvented itself. By the late 1990s, major British television channels were commissioning lavishly funded programmes from hyper-diffusionists. And, for the first time, archaeologists and historians began to feel that what was previously a joke genre was undermining their work.

The architect of the new cult archaeology was Graham Hancock, a former East African correspondent of the *Economist*. He is, at heart, an extreme hyperdiffusionist; but his rhetoric is ingenious, and reminiscent of 'Creation scientists' who use real gaps in the fossil record as a subtle way of introducing their young-earth belief system. Hancock's 1995 book *Fingerprints of the Gods* was built around what appeared, at the time, to be a tantalizing archaeological mystery. In 1990, Professor Robert Schoch, a scientist with a PhD in geology who teaches at Boston University, investigated the geology of the Great Sphinx of Giza and found evidence of prolonged water erosion. He concluded that the severity of this erosion pointed to a construction not later than 5000 BC, which would make the Sphinx older than the ancient Egyptian civilization.[13] So, if the Egyptians didn't build the Sphinx, who did? Schoch's findings inspired Hancock to build a master-theory that would tie up all manner of archaeological anomalies. According to *Fingerprints of the Gods*, the Great

Sphinx, the Andean temples of Tiahuanco, and Mexico's Pyramids of the Sun and Moon, 'reveal not only the clear fingerprints of an unknown people who flourished during the last ice age, but also disquieting signs of high intelligence and scientific knowledge'.

In other words, this is basically *Chariots of the Gods?* without the spacemen; its conclusion – that the remains of Atlantis lie buried under the Antarctic – is no more credible than the theories of von Däniken. But it was not the Antarctic theory that persuaded 5 million people to buy *Fingerprints of the Gods*: it was the Sphinx. I remember a tenured professor at a leading American university telling me: 'Obviously a lot of what Hancock says is rubbish, but you can't dismiss the stuff about the Sphinx so easily. There is clearly a case to answer.'

He was right: there *was* a case to answer, if only because Egyptian archaeological sites were swarming with amateur scholars hoping to be the next Graham Hancock. Professional geologists (of whom Schoch is not one – he actually teaches general studies at Boston University) took another look at the heavy erosion at the base of the Sphinx and came up with several perfectly plausible explanations, such as the poor quality of the limestone, which did not involve dismantling the entire history of ancient Egypt. To put it another way, they used Occam's razor.[14] But, by that stage, Hancock had a contract for a TV series in the bag.

In 2003, *The Da Vinci Code* brought every pseudo-historian out of the woodwork. A lot had happened since the first publication of *The Holy Blood and the Holy Grail* in 1982. The genre had grown enormously, for a start. After *Fingerprints of the Gods*, bookshops filled up with titles exploring the hidden links between Egyptian religion, Neolithic monuments, Freemasonry and the Great Flood. One pair of authors, Christopher Knight and Robert Lomas, actually managed to tie together all four. Meanwhile, proper biblical scholars had been making genuinely exciting discoveries that sent pseudohistorians who could not read a word of New Testament Greek into a feeding frenzy.

In the last twenty years, researchers have unearthed new information about Jewish, Christian and Gnostic beliefs in the first, second and third centuries AD. An excellent summary of these discoveries is *Lost Christianities* (2003), by the New Testament specialist Bart Ehrman, who investigates the obscure late 'Gospels' attributed to Peter, Philip, Mary Magdalene and others.[15] With the possible exception of the Gnostic Gospel of Thomas, these texts were written far too late to tell us anything about the historical Jesus. But, because they were championed by heretical sects, they were suppressed by the early church. Dan Brown weaves this detail into *The Da Vinci Code*, but grossly inflates the number of texts and claims that they reveal Jesus's marriage to Mary Magdalene. (As Ehrman points out, none of them says anything of the sort.[16])

Bogus historians, needless to say, have had a field day. Laurence Gardner has taken time off from his duties as Jacobite Historiographer Royal and Presidential Attaché to the European Court of Princes to write *The Magdalene Legacy* (2005), an account of the marriage of Jesus and Mary at Cana, together with 'detective work' on the paintings of Leonardo. The book relocates the burial place of Jesus from Jerusalem to Qumran, though it also leaves open the possibility that he was buried in India. Not so long ago, it would have been self-published; now it appears under the imprint of Rupert Murdoch's HarperElement.

The same publisher is responsible for *The Jesus Papers* (2006) by Michael Baigent, which uses recent research to make a more complex and authoritative-sounding case for Jesus's marriage to Mary Magdalene and his contact with Egyptian mysticism. The book is pseudohistory from beginning to end. The 'Jesus papers' are supposedly letters from Jesus to the Sanhedrin in which he denies his divinity; at one stage, Baigent is shown the original glass-covered papyrus documents by an unnamed Israeli businessman, and is even allowed to hold them in his hand ('I was awestruck and speechless'). Alas, they disappear before he can have them translated.[17] I picked up my copy of Baigent's book in the religion section of a well-known bookshop, next to similarly packaged but factual and properly sourced books about recent biblical discoveries.

In the history section of the same shop, meanwhile,

I found the paperback edition of *Talisman: Sacred Cities, Secret Faith* by Graham Hancock and his fellow cult archaeologist Robert Bauval. This densely annotated volume, looking far more like a conventional history book than Hancock's previous work, pieces together the story of a 'secret religion' founded in ancient Egypt that developed into Gnosticism, Hermetic mysticism and Freemasonry, and culminated in the Zionist-Masonic project to found the state of Israel. Finally, Hancock and Bauval suggest that the two pillars of Solomon's Temple and the Star of David represented in Masonic art bear a strong resemblance to the Twin Towers and the Pentagon – in other words, that the atrocities of 11 September 2001 are pieces in their jigsaw puzzle.[18] (Quite how, they do not explain.) When I came across this passage, with its resonances of anti-Semitic conspiracy literature, I checked the spine of the book to remind myself of the publisher: it was the main imprint of Penguin Books.

Recent titles by Baigent and Hancock and Bauval may carry some of the trappings of academia, but one could argue that anyone familiar with their track record, or who devoted just a few minutes to examining their claims, would approach their books with extreme suspicion. The disturbing thing is that the blurring of history and pseudo-history goes beyond the attempts by cult archaeologists with 'form' to reinvent themselves as scholars.

For a demonstration of how fine the line between

archaeology and cult archaeology has become, try comparing two apparently similar books, covering the same period and aimed at the same market: *Lost Civilizations of the Stone Age* by Richard Rudgley (1998) and *Europe's Lost Civilization* (2004) by Peter Marshall. Rudgley argues that, thousands of years before the Sumerians, Neolithic man had evolved a literate society that practised rug-making, dentistry and accountancy. Marshall thinks the builders of the megaliths were a highly advanced civilization with a grasp of astronomy, philosophy, science and seafaring. Both books contain fascinating, properly footnoted data about the Stone Age; both put forward controversial points of view.

It takes a few minutes to work out that, while Rudgley makes tentative suggestions based firmly on data, giving due weight to other academic points of view, Marshall draws heavily on his imagination and peppers his text with faulty inferences. He argues, for example, that the equal spacing of stones at Carnac in Brittany shows that 'clearly, the megalith builders were masters of geometry and mathematics';[19] and, like several hyperdiffusionists before him, he offers his own experiences of sailing a small boat as proof of ancient maritime prowess. Marshall, in short, is a cult archaeologist, yet his publishers, Hodder Headline, officially categorize his work as history. (They also publish a book, *History and Historians* by John Warren, which offers a framework for evaluating historians and discusses 'the distortion of history as myth'.)

The most remarkable triumph of the new historical counterknowledge, however, is Gavin Menzies's best-selling *1421: The Year China Discovered the World* (2002). Menzies, a former Royal Navy submarine commander, argues that vast Chinese fleets circumnavigated the globe in the early fifteenth century, landing or establishing colonies in Australia, New Zealand, Greenland, Massachusetts, the Caribbean and Brazil. As Menzies puts it: 'These remarkable Chinese admirals rounded the Cape of Good Hope 66 years before Dias, passed through the Strait of Magellan 98 years before Magellan, surveyed Australia three centuries before Captain Cook, Antarctica and the Arctic four centuries before the first European, and America 70 years before Columbus.'[20] On the way, they introduced sea otters to New Zealand, horses to America, chickens to South America and coffee to Puerto Rico.

Or perhaps not. The reviews of *1421* by professional historians were sceptical, to put it mildly. 'The drivel of a two-year-old,' was the verdict of the leading British historian Felipe Fernández-Armesto, professor of global environmental history at Queen Mary, University of London.[21] Many other scholars expressed essentially the same view, only in more polite language. 'Menzies flouts the basic rules of both historical study and elementary logic,' wrote Robert Finlay in the *Journal of World History*. 'He misrepresents the scholarship of others, and he frequently fails to cite those from whom he borrows . . .

His misunderstanding of the nature of [Chinese imperial] ships impels him to depict voyages no captain would attempt and no mariner would survive.'[22] Yet, five years after *1421* had been comprehensively exposed as garbage, an updated paperback edition of the book was being specially promoted by *all* of Britain's leading chains of bookstores.

How could this happen? For once, we can answer this question confidently, since in 2006 an investigative documentary by the Australian Broadcasting Corporation revealed exactly how the book was fabricated: it really is a scandalous story, which we shall look at in detail in chapter five. The point I want to make here is that Menzies has been partly insulated from criticism because *1421*, like so much modern counterknowledge, fits neatly into someone else's agenda. Menzies's theory goes down a treat in China, where he has been invited to address universities and his supporters include senior Communist Party officials. In 2003, President Hu Jintao, on a visit to Australia, told a joint session of parliament: 'Back in the 1420s the expeditionary fleet of China's Ming dynasty reached Australian shores.'[23] Presumably he picked up this fantastic idea from Menzies.

Modern historians work hard to avoid the nationalist, ethnic, political or religious bias that coloured the work of previous generations. The new pseudohistorians, in contrast, are reinvigorating these old prejudices. The work of Baigent, for example, is coloured by a hatred of the

Roman Catholic Church modelled on old-fashioned anti-Catholic propaganda. And, as we saw earlier, Hancock and Bauval's belief in a Zionist-Masonic 'project', though couched in the most careful terms, carries overtones of sinister conspiracy literature.

Still, at least this material is not taught in schools or universities (though the job of teachers is made more difficult by their students' preference for exciting bogus history above the real, more prosaic kind). But one variety of pseudohistory has worked its way into school textbooks and university curricula; its practitioners hold leading teaching positions at respected institutions. It's called Afrocentric history, and anyone who criticizes it runs a high risk of being accused of racism. Which is ironic, really, since much Afrocentric scholarship is racist counter-knowledge.

In 2007, Routledge, one of the leading academic publishers in Britain and America, published *The History of Africa* by Molefi Kete Asante, professor of African-American studies at Temple University, Philadelphia. Professor Asante (born Arthur Lee Smith, Jr.) is the author of sixty-three books, including a high-school textbook. His new book is intended as a standard text for undergraduates on both sides of the Atlantic. What should alarm us is that its account of early African history is rooted in pseudohistory.

For Asante, Africa is not just the birthplace of *Homo*

sapiens but also, more controversially, of civilization. Asante always uses the Egyptian word *'Kemet'* for ancient Egypt, explaining that it meant 'land of the blacks' or 'the black country'.[24] In fact, it meant only the latter, and in a restricted sense: *kemet* (black) refers to the fertile soil, as opposed to *deshret* (red), the desert. Asante is implying that the Egyptians defined themselves in terms of their skin colour, which is not true.

He goes on to state baldly that *'Kemet'* invented writing and architecture, both very dubious claims. On the subject of the architect Imhotep, who lived around 2700 BC, he writes: 'He was the first philosopher in human history . . . As the first human being to be deified, that is made a deity by his society, he stands at the very top of African and world philosophy so great were his deeds.'[25] No source for this information is given. Actually, we know virtually nothing about the real Imhotep beyond the fact that he designed the step pyramid at Saqqara; he left no writings or authentic sayings, there are no eyewitness accounts of him, and his deification did not take place until 2,000 years after his death. Elsewhere, Asante claims that 'both Hannibal and St Augustine were black Africans. No question about it.' Yet Hannibal was a Phoenician of Semitic ancestry and Augustine a Berber; neither was unquestionably an ethnic black African.[26]

What sort of history professor can get away with such sloppiness? The answer is, an Afrocentric professor who does not believe that 'African' historians (by which he means anyone of African ancestry, however distant) should be constrained by 'European' conventions (by which he means methodological rigour). Moreover, Asante holds extreme views about the right of white professors to teach black American history: they can only do so if they work from an African-American perspective. Most white professors 'do not have the proper orientation to adequately teach any African-American studies,' he writes. 'They tend to be off on either orientation, facts, pedagogical skill, or humility.'[27] Try switching round 'black' and 'white' and substituting 'European' for 'African-American' and it becomes clear what a breathtakingly racist position this is.

Asante's *History of Africa* opens with a hymn of praise to its dedicatee, 'the Senegalese genius Cheikh Anta Diop ... who proposed the important thesis that Africa was not only the cradle of humanity but also the cradle of civilization'.[28] Indeed, such is Asante's debt to Diop that he describes himself as a 'Diopist'. And that rather gives the game away. Diop (1923–86), a controversial historian and anthropologist, argued that the rulers of ancient Egypt were all Negroes, a view that is rejected by most specialists in the field. He also put forward the pseudohistorical thesis that 'Athens was founded by a colony of Black Egyptians'.[29]

Some American academics have been horrified by this politically motivated reinvention of ancient history. In her book *Not Out of Africa* (1996), the eminent classical historian

Mary Lefkowitz comprehensively demolished the theories of Diop and his better-known contemporary, Martin Bernal, author of *Black Athena*. Lefkowitz, former Andrew W. Mellon professor in the humanities at Wellesley College, Massachusetts, says there is not the slightest evidence that the Greeks stole their philosophy from Egypt. She has also criticized Asante for implying that 'being an African enables one to know about the particulars of African history, simply by intuition or osmosis'.[30]

In Lefkowitz's view, Afrocentrism is a political rather than a scholarly project. 'In effect, Afrocentrists are demanding that ordinary historical methodology be discarded in favour of a system of their own choosing,' she writes. 'This system allows them to ignore chronology and facts if they are inconvenient for their purposes. In other words, their historical methodology allows them to alter the course of history in order to meet their own specific needs.'[31]

Afrocentrism has its black opponents too, who object to the way young black people are being drawn into a quasi-religious movement. Clarence Walker, professor of history at the University of California at Davis, writes that: 'Like religion, Afrocentrism operates in the realm of faith and belief. One either accepts its preposterous claims or is anathematized. Doubters are either racist, if they are white, or inauthentically black and co-opted by a world of Eurocentric madness.'[32]

It is this element of moral blackmail that distinguishes Afrocentrism from other forms of historical counter-knowledge. Routledge prides itself on its rigour; I find it hard to believe that it would allow a scholar to make the sweeping and unsupported statements that we find in Asante's *History of Africa*, which is supposed to be a basic textbook, unless it was afraid of being accused of racism.

Whatever the explanation, the reality is that a leading academic publisher has added to the mountain of books that make claims the falsehood of which could have been established if an editor had spent just a few minutes checking the sources. *A History of Africa, The Holy Blood and the Holy Grail, The Jesus Papers, Talisman, 1421* and countless other titles all do the same thing, to a greater or lesser extent. They employ the rhetoric of authentic history, but not its method, to present as fact the sort of myths that, until a few years ago, no one outside the cultic milieu took seriously.

Plenty of people object to the idea that any history can be described as authentic. Authenticity is a slippery concept, they say. It is dependent on notions of correct historical method that, to a far greater degree than in the natural sciences, reflect the shifting beliefs and interests of an intellectual elite. To which one can only reply: that's true up to a point, but the first duty of the scholar is to report things that did, rather than didn't, happen. In the words of one historian:

With regard to my factual reporting of the events of the war, I have made it a principle not to write down the first story that came my way, and not even to be guided by my own general impressions; either I was present myself at the events which I have described or else I heard of them from eyewitnesses whose reports I have checked with as much thoroughness as possible. Not that, even then, the truth was easy to discover . . . and it may well be that my history will seem less easy to read because of the absence of a romantic element. It will be enough for me, however, if these words of mine are judged useful by those who want to understand clearly the events that happened in the past.[33]

That was Thucydides, writing about the Peloponnesian War. Little did he know that, 2,400 years later, he would share a publisher with Graham Hancock.

4

Desperate Remedies

The quack doctors of Georgian England were shameless liars and self-publicists. If their advertisements were to be believed, no medical condition was so serious, or so trivial, that their pills and potions could not cure it. Bromfield's Pills Against All Diseases promised to eradicate 'Giddiness in the Head, sudden Flushings, Putrification and Stinking of the Gums, Tooth-ach, Stinking-breath and thick Vapours arising from HYPOCHONDRIA to the Midriff'. A physician in High Holborn sold medicine that would cure not only 'Pain in the Head and Stomack' but also red hair and freckles.[1]

The quacks invoked science, not faith healing or magic. And, as time went on, they took to 'graduating themselves' with phoney degrees and professional qualifications from institutions of their own invention.[2] By the early nineteenth century, writes Roy Porter in his book *Quacks*, the medical profession (such as it was) found itself attacked by 'swarms of sharp operators – untrained druggists, irregulars and itinerants, all making their pile'. They were driven out of mainstream medicine only after a long campaign by the surgeon Thomas Wakley, who used his journal, the *Lancet*, to attack 'the satanic system of quackery'. Wakley was particularly angry at the way respectable bodies toyed with the 'pest' of bogus medicine; he described the College of Physicians as 'vile', the Corporation of Surgeons as 'Bats', and the Society of Apothecaries as 'the Hags of Rhubarb Hall'. The *Lancet* specialized in revealing the secret ingredients of patent medicines and inviting readers to expose their local quacks. And, eventually, the strategy paid off, though it was not until the Pharmacy Act of 1868 that quacks were legally forbidden to sell poisons and addictive drugs to the public.[3]

If Wakley could come back today, what would he think? He would be astonished, of course, by the conquest of nearly every disease that had ravaged his patients. But suppose that, having absorbed the miracles of modern science, he then investigated 'alternative medicine'. He might well ask: why, when you have achieved all this, do you still tolerate quacks? Why do millions of people buy their books and useless sugar pills? Why do you employ them in your health service? Why do your governments listen to their advice? Why is this pest taught in universities?

At the beginning of the twenty-first century, quackery is making ever deeper inroads into healthcare. An industry worth billions of pounds is built around treatments or therapies that are based on claims that can be shown to be false or for which there is no evidence. This is counterknowledge, in other words; and, like other purveyors of counterknowledge, quacks range from true believers to fraudsters. Most of them occupy territory somewhere in between and fit into Harry Frankfurt's category of the bullshitter: someone who adopts a casual approach to the truth.

Nearly all quacks shelter under the umbrella of complementary and alternative medicine, often referred to as CAM. (Significantly, despite decades of debate, there is no agreed definition of CAM, or of the difference between 'complementary' and 'alternative' therapies.) This is a good choice of hiding place. Short of making a racist joke, there is probably no quicker way to sour the atmosphere at a London dinner party than to question the value of alternative medicine. Nonetheless, the simple truth is that most such medicine is 'alternative' for a good reason: it doesn't work.

Dr Arnold Relman, a former Harvard professor of medicine and editor of the *New England Journal of Medicine*, elegantly dismantled the whole idea of 'alternative' medicine in an article for the *New Republic* in 1998. He wrote: 'There are not two kinds of medicine, one conventional and the other unconventional, that can be practiced jointly in a new kind of "integrative medicine". Nor . . . are there two kinds of thinking, or two ways to find out which treatments work and which do not. In the best kind of medical practice, all kinds of treatment must be tested objectively. In the end there will only be those that pass the test and those that do not, those that are proven worthwhile and those that are not.'[4]

Raymond Tallis, professor emeritus of geriatric medicine at the University of Manchester and a distinguished philosopher, makes a similar point: 'Alternative medicine is the kind of medicine people took when there was no alternative; when there were no antibiotics, no steroids, no effective treatments for cancer, heart attacks, stomach ulcers.'[5]

Relman and Tallis are not denying the existence of grey areas; there can be a lot of confusion while we wait to see if a treatment passes the appropriate tests. Our judgement of whether it is 'worthwhile', whether a patient will benefit from it in some way, will often be subjective. In contrast, our judgement of whether a claim is *true* should be objective, based on an impartial reading of data, even if we later have to revise our judgement as new facts emerge.

Identifying bogus medical claims is usually more straightforward than identifying bogus history. You subject treatment X and treatment Y to a rigorous comparison. Where drugs or 'natural' food supplements are concerned, this comparison often takes the form a randomized double-blind test in which neither evaluator nor subject knows which is which. X might be a drug or food supplement you want to test, Y a sugar pill. If X beats the placebo, then scientists have to begin the tricky process of evaluating the result. If, on the other hand, it performs no better than the placebo, then you can usually say with some confidence: 'X doesn't work.'

Alternative and traditional medicines don't beat the placebo; that's why they remain alternative and traditional, rather than part of orthodox medicine. On the other hand, they may well match a placebo in effectiveness; and the placebo effect, as any GP will tell you, can be freakishly powerful. About 30 per cent of patients in clinical trials feel better after taking placebos in the form of dummy pills or saline injections. In the words of Dr Robert DeLap of the US Food and Drug Administration: 'Expectation is a powerful thing. The more you believe you're going to benefit from a treatment, the more likely it is that you will experience a benefit.'[6]

The reason unorthodox medicines, supplements and therapies so often match the placebo effect is simple: they *are* placebos. If a man takes a pill containing powdered rhino horn for erectile dysfunction (a traditional African remedy) and ends up with a rhino-sized erection, it is his brain that has done the work, not the ingredients. If, however, he gets the same result after taking Viagra, that is almost certainly because the drug sildenafil citrate has increased the blood flow into his penis. Viagra works, and Pfizer, who make it, can justifiably say so. The rhino pill manufacturers can only truthfully say that their product may possibly have a beneficial effect – but *not as a result of anything that the product contains*. And the same goes for the manufacturers of thousands of herbal remedies and food supplements.

The problem is that most suppliers of 'alternative' medicines and therapies aren't interested in what they can truthfully claim: they are interested in what they can get away with claiming, which is a different matter. And they can get away with a lot, because so many of us have lost confidence in the safety net of conventional medicine.

Although people in the West are actually healthier than ever before, their expectations of good health are rising faster than the ability of scientists, doctors or politicians to deliver it. There has been no medical breakthrough in the last twenty years to compare with the discovery of antibiotics or the link between smoking and lung cancer. Pharmaceutical companies invest millions of pounds in drugs that have only a marginal effect on our health; according to GlaxoSmithKline, 90 per cent of new drugs work in only 30 to 50 per cent of patients.[7] The British government pumps extra billions into primary care without achieving a significant rise in consumer satisfaction; overall, improvements in medical care advance inch by inch, through trial and error.

Confronted by the anxieties of the 'worried well', the most intellectually honest scientists and doctors – that is, those whose approach is evidence-based – are reduced to offering simple advice that works: eat plenty of fruit and vegetables, take regular exercise – and that's about it. Individuals can take steps to reduce their risk of coronary heart disease and cancer, but 'healthy living' does not guarantee a healthy life. The relationship between lifestyle and health is mysterious; GPs are more sensitive than they used to be to the psychological components of illness and take these into account when making a diagnosis. But the vast majority do not attempt to micromanage the behaviour of people who already eat and exercise reasonably sensibly, because they know that it is unlikely to achieve anything.

Alternative medicine, on the other hand, recognizes almost no limits to what it can achieve. It feeds on middle-class anxieties about body image, diet, lifestyle and illness, offering healing therapies at every level from the cellular to the cosmic. The following is a list of a few well-known CAM therapies, with some indication as to the empirical foundation of their claims.

Acupuncture: Everyone 'knows' that this traditional Chinese practice actually works for the control of chronic pain. Or does it? In 1990, three Dutch epidemiologists analysed fifty-one controlled studies of acupuncture for chronic pain and found that the evidence was 'doubtful'; they also found no evidence that acupuncture is better than a placebo at treating addiction.[8] In 2004, scientists at the University of Heidelberg cast doubt on the usefulness of acupuncture for controlling post-operative nausea, one of the few alleged benefits supported in scientific journals. In short, the effectiveness of acupuncture other than as a placebo is still unproven.

Aromatherapy: This is the therapeutic use of essential oils from flowers, trees, shrubs and their fruits, blooms, leaves and roots. Some advocates of the 'science' of aromatherapy claim that the odours can revitalize cells, calm nerves, nourish the skin and boost the immune system. Not one peer-reviewed paper supports any of these claims. Essentials oils are placebos that smell nice.

Chinese medicine: the notion that the herbal remedies, massages and needle therapy of traditional Chinese medicine (TCM) constitute a parallel system of healthcare that complements Western methods is gaining ground all the time; but not as a result of peer-reviewed research data. The most recent large-scale review of randomized controlled trials of TCM, published by the *British Medical Journal* in 1999, found that, of nearly 3,000 trials, only 15 per cent were blinded, sample sizes were small, effectiveness was rarely quantitatively expressed, and 'most trials claimed that the tested treatments were effective, indicating that publication bias may be common'.[9] By 2007, only one Chinese-developed drug, the anti-malarial plant extract artemisinin, had received preliminary approval from the World Health Organization.[10]

Chiropractic: This is a form of alternative medicine that aims to improve general bodily health by manipulating the spine. It was invented in 1895 by Daniel David Palmer, a grocer and 'magnetic healer', who believed that 95 per cent of all diseases were caused by 'subluxation' (partial dislocation) of the spine.[11] Traditional chiropractors still believe that most physical disease can be attributed to these subluxations. There is no scientific evidence to support this notion.

Craniosacral therapy (CST): This is based on the belief that the human brain makes rhythmic movements at a rate of 10–14 per minute, which are independent of breathing or heart rate. Diseases can be detected by aberrations in this rhythm, it is claimed. Moreover, CST therapists applying very light pressure to the head can improve the functioning of the central nervous system and bolster resistance to disease. The International Alliance of Healthcare Educators, a Florida-based charity that promotes CST, maintains that the therapy can be used to treat autism, traumatic brain injuries, learning disabilities, neurovascular disorders and post-traumatic stress disorder.[12] The only snag is that the craniosacral rhythm does not, in fact, exist and therefore, unsurprisingly, CST therapists examining the same patient have detected quite different 'rhythms'.[13]

Detox diets: The notion that depriving your body of various foodstuffs removes poisons from it is a fiction, and a potentially dangerous one. According to the British Dietetic

Association, the word 'detox' is meaningless. The body contains its own 'detoxifiers' in the form of the liver, kidneys, skin, intestines and lungs; they don't need any special help to do their job. Diets based on the concept are a marketing myth and often encourage people to cut out important food groups.[14] Scientists at the University of Southern California have concluded that the arguments for detox diets are 'categorically unsubstantiated and run counter to our understanding of human physiology and biochemistry'. Teenagers and pregnant women are particularly at risk from this fad.[15]

Homeopathy: This early nineteenth-century form of quackery teaches that substances become more powerful the more they are diluted. It has been described (with good reason) as alternative medicine's ultimate fake; yet, as we shall see when we look at homeopathy later, it is entrenched in the National Health Service and in the past decade has been taken up by universities.

Reflexology: This massage therapy is based on the theory that each body part is reflected on the hands and feet, and that pressing on specific areas of these can have therapeutic effects in other parts of the body. There is no scientific evidence to show that such a link exists.

It's worth noting that these and dozens of other alternative therapies are based on mutually exclusive theories about the human body. Traditional chiropractors and reflexologists have quite different ideas about how the body works. The former believe that the well-being of the whole body is essentially dependent on a spine free of 'subluxations'. The latter believe that pressure to the soles of the feet triggers (undetectable) signals to different organs through the peripheral nervous system. Although both chiropractic and reflexology are equally useless as diagnostic tools, they are based on quite different physiological 'charts' and therefore contradict each other. But that does not worry most consumers of alternative medicine or, it seems, many of its providers.

CAM knows its market: its books, diets and potions are targeted at people with a short attention span who will soon be grazing elsewhere. Hence the constant need to come up with new products. Differences are played down in order to present a united front against 'blinkered' conventional medicine. Interestingly, you can find a similar camaraderie of counterknowledge in cult archaeology. An author who believes that Stonehenge was built by Aztecs will cheerfully recommend the work of someone who thinks it was built by the Priory of Sion, because they both recognize their real enemy as orthodox scholarship.

Complementary and alternative medicine provides what sociologists call a 'plausibility structure' for the myriad unproven medical claims that come under its umbrella. In the world of CAM, cranial osteopaths, Native American shamans and Chinese herbalists can all claim to tap into a nebulous 'wisdom'; and to attack the empirical basis of this wisdom is regarded as narrow-minded or bad manners.

The growing influence of CAM in Western society can be illustrated by looking at two manifestations of bogus medicine: homeopathy and nutritionism. The former dates back 200 years, the latter less than a couple of decades; both of them fall into the category of counterknowledge.

Homeopathy involves giving sick patients very small doses of substances called 'remedies' which are supposed to produce the same or similar symptoms of illness in healthy people if given in larger doses. This seeks to stimulate the body's defence mechanisms and processes in order to prevent or treat illness. That, incidentally, is the short definition of homeopathy given by the US National Center for Complementary and Alternative Medicine.[16] Yet even this thoroughly sympathetic body (funded by the American taxpayer) cannot avoid making homeopathy sound like nineteenth-century quackery, because that is exactly what it is.

The principles of homeopathy were devised by Samuel Hahnemann (1755–1843), a German physician who believed that chronic diseases were manifestations of a suppressed itch. His 'law of infinitesimals' stated that the smaller the dose of the 'remedy', the more powerful the effect. Homeopathic potions dilute the original substance (a herb or mineral) so completely that it disappears. My local chemist, for example, sells homeopathic sulphur tablets marked '30C': that means that the proportion of sulphur to the inactive substance is 1 to 100.[30] That's why there is no mention of sulphur in the ingredients on the container: the pill doesn't contain any.

Admittedly, modern homeopaths spend a lot of time engaging in a form of psychotherapy with their patients, asking them about the emotional stresses in their lives in order to refine their diagnosis. Also, inevitably, they embroider their theories with references to quantum physics. But the core teaching of homeopathy has remained the same for 200 years. Bishop William Croswell Doane (1832–1913), the first Episcopalian bishop of Albany, New York, summed it up as follows:

> Stir the mixture well
> Lest it prove inferior,
> Then put half a drop
> Into Lake Superior.
> Every other day
> Take a drop in water,
> You'll be better soon
> Or at least you oughter.

The poet and physician Oliver Wendell Holmes (1809–94), addressing a class of graduating medical students in 1871, warned them against 'that parody of medieval theology' represented by the doctrine of dilutions. Even in the nineteenth century, sensible people knew that homeopathy was as scientifically rigorous as reading tea leaves.

Let's stick with that analogy. Imagine that the art of tea-leaf reading, known as tasseography,[17] was held in high regard by members of the British royal family; and that, thanks to royal patronage, at the beginning of the twenty-first century the National Health Service was funding five hospitals based around the supposed diagnostic power of tea leaves. Then imagine that, despite indisputable evidence suggesting that such power does not exist, six British universities were offering degrees in tasseography.

Substitute homeopathy for tasseography, and the picture is accurate: five hospitals, six university degrees, all of them built on a foundation of antiquated but thriving pseudoscience. One of the reasons it is thriving is the royal family's support for homeopathy, which dates back to the 1830s.

The current Prince of Wales has founded a charity, the Prince's Foundation for Integrated Health, which tells the public that homeopathy is 'used to treat chronic conditions such as asthma; eczema; arthritis; fatigue disorders like ME; headache and migraine; menstrual and menopausal problems; irritable bowel syndrome; Crohn's disease; allergies; repeated ear, nose, throat and chest infections or urine infections; depression and anxiety'.

The distinguished pharmacologist Professor David Colquhoun of University College London points out that the foundation gives no indication as to whether these treatments work. 'That is just irresponsible,' he says. 'And to describe pills that contain no trace of the substance on the label as "very diluted" [as the foundation does] is plain dishonest.'[18] To put it bluntly, Prince Charles is abusing his constitutional position to foist bad science on his future subjects.

'Homeopathy is to medicine what astrology is to astronomy,' says Michael Baum, professor emeritus of surgery at University College London. 'It's witchcraft – totally barmy, totally refuted, and yet it's available on the NHS.'[19]

Moreover, homeopathy enjoys cross-party support. In 2007, a House of Commons early day motion seeking to protect NHS expenditure on homeopathic hospitals was supported by MPs from all the major parties; a Conservative spokesman said that homeopathy was 'valuable' and should form part of a 'patient-led' health service.[20] In other words, if there is enough demand for treatments based on a complete fiction, then the taxpayer should subsidize them.

The Labour government, meanwhile, has encouraged the spread of homeopathy and other CAM remedies to Northern Ireland. In February 2007, Peter Hain, the secretary of state, pumped £200,000 of public money into making homeopathy, acupuncture and massage more available to NHS practices in Londonderry and Belfast. Colquhoun commented: 'Peter Hain used to be something of a hero to me. In the 70s his work for the anti-apartheid movement was an inspiration. Now he has sunk to promoting junk science. Very sad.'[21]

Homeopathy has been available on the NHS since it was set up in 1948. It is only in the last ten years, however, that publicly funded British universities have started offering courses and BSc degrees in homeopathy. The existence of these degrees was not widely known until a special report in the journal *Nature* appeared in March 2007. The report's author, Jim Giles, discovered that two of the six universities offering homoeopathy degrees, the University of Central Lancashire and the University of Salford, refused to discuss them or even reveal the content of the courses. Professor Colquhoun has experienced the same problem and is trying to use freedom of information legislation to extract the details.

The *Nature* report also found that 'academic' homeopaths are actively resisting the best mechanism to test their propositions, the randomized double-blind clinical trial. 'Trying to do what I do in that context didn't work very well,' said Clare Relton, a homeopath conducting research at the University of Sheffield. She believes that homeopathy is scientific, but that double-blind tests in which the patient knows there is a chance of receiving a placebo break down the necessary trust. She and other homeopaths prefer to rely on 'more qualitative methods, such as case studies and non-blinded comparisons of treatment options'.[22]

How can a university get away with offering a degree in 200-year-old quackery? Part of the answer is that homeopathy is taught alongside other varieties of medical counterknowledge that act as camouflage; the universities in question also teach aromatherapy, acupuncture, traditional Chinese medicine, herbal medicine, reflexology, osteopathy, therapeutic bodywork, naturopathy, Ayurveda, shiatsu and qigong. 'None of these is, by any stretch of the imagination, science,' wrote David Colquhoun in *Nature*, 'yet they form part of BSc degrees. They are not being taught as part of cultural history, or as odd sociological phenomena, but as science.'[23]

Perhaps the most important example of the blurring of the boundaries of medical science is the rise of the media nutritionists. Advice on nutrition used to be dispensed mainly by registered dieticians – state-registered members of the British or American Dietetic Associations with proper science degrees. Dieticians know a lot about the effect of various foods on the human body, and it is precisely because they are aware that the links between diet and mortality rates are so tenuous that their advice is so simple and unexciting. Their basic message is the same as that of doctors: eat a balanced diet with lots of fruit and veg.

Then at some point in the 1990s the new nutritionists arrived – on daytime television, in health food stores, in the health sections of bookshops, and, as the phenomenon gathered pace, in supermarkets, the tabloid newspapers, the bestseller lists and on prime-time TV. These diet specialists belong to the world of complementary and alternative medicine, but there is nothing 'alternative' about their marketing skills.

Dr Gillian McKeith, a bossy Scottish nutritionist, has sold more than a million copies of her book *You Are What You Eat*, which was also the most borrowed book from British libraries in 2005–6; her hit television programme of the same name, in which 'overeaters are trained in Gillian's healthy ways', has run to several series and airs in fourteen countries. Her career was going swimmingly, in fact, until she attracted the attention of Ben Goldacre, a young hospital doctor who writes the Bad Science column in the *Guardian*, who decided to find out more about her doctorate and discovered that it was awarded by a non-accredited American institution on the basis of a correspondence course.[24]

News of Goldacre's discovery spread like wildfire, and McKeith's career has never quite recovered from this humiliation; but most media nutritionists have not been exposed to any scrutiny and still exude plausibility. They are careful not to come across as New Age fruitcakes. They do not promise to realign our biorhythms on the astral plane; they talk about 'The Health Remedies in your Fruit Bowl', to quote the title of an article by Angela Dowden, registered nutritionist and former Health Writer of the Year. She says: 'Whichever fruit you fancy, you can be sure you'll get a healthy boost of fibre, vitamins and disease-preventive antioxidants. But fruit is also nature's pharmacist – so by selecting carefully, your fruit bowl can become a valuable source of home remedies for minor ailments.'

Dowden gives an example. For eye-strain, take bilberries. 'These European cousins of American blueberries contain anthocyanin antioxidants which strengthen the blood vessels supplying the retina in the eye. Bilberry extracts have been shown to treat visual fatigue caused by prolonged reading and working in dim light.'[25]

Dowden's tone is so cheerful and reasonable that it seems positively rude to ask: 'Shown by whom?' But it's a good question. Goldacre read this passage and worked his way through all the references to bilberries in medical journals. There was no evidence to suggest that bilberries had the slightest effect on the retina. 'I read 84 very boring abstracts to make sure,' he writes. He describes Dowden's claims as 'fairly typical media nutritionist fare – and horseshit, as media nutritionist fare usually is'.[26]

This 'fare' has not only gone down extremely well with the public; in the process, it has also pushed the boring but accurate claims of qualified dieticians to the margins. Anyone can call himself a nutritionist. Patrick Holford, founder of the Institute for Optimum Nutrition, is Britain's most influential nutritionist. His *Optimum Nutrition Bible* has sold half a million copies, and he has advised the National Association of Head Teachers, the Food Standards Agency and the Prince of Wales' Foundation. In 2007, he was made a visiting professor in nutrition at the University of Teesside. Yet his only academic qualification is an undergraduate degree in psychology from York University (though he does hold a diploma from his own institute). The barrier for becoming an 'expert' is set so low that the only real requirement is a talent for self-promotion.

Media nutritionists cannot easily be identified as quacks because so much of what they say seems innocuous. 'Fruit is nature's pharmacist,' insists Dowden. (It isn't, actually, but it's a nice thought.) Instead of New Age mumbo-jumbo, they produce quasi-scientific statements about 'the link between' natural food supplements and various manifestations of good health. They refer confidently to clinical trials and employ many of the buzz-words used by doctors: such and such a substance is 'rich in antioxidants, which have been shown to prevent cancer'. But what they are actually doing, most of the time, is manipulating the language and literature of medicine.

'The scholarliness of her work is a thing to behold,' says Goldacre of Gillian McKeith. 'She produces lengthy documents that have an air of "referenciness", with nice little superscript numbers, which talk about trials, and studies, and research, and papers . . . but when you follow the numbers, and check the references, it's shocking how often they aren't what she claimed them to be in the main body of the text. Or they refer to funny little magazines and books, such as *Delicious*, *Creative Living*, *Healthy Eating*, and my favourite, *Spiritual Nutrition and the Rainbow Diet*, rather than proper academic journals.'[27]

In an article for the *British Medical Journal*, Goldacre discussed media nutritionists in general: 'The whole field is based on a small palette of simple academic errors. Food gurus extrapolate wildly, creating hypotheses from metabolism flow charts or interesting theoretical laboratory bench data, and then using them to justify a clinical intervention ... Similarly, the media nutritionists extrapolate from observational data to giving 'evidence based' interventional advice.'[28]

Media nutritionists often dispense counterknowledge, and people act on their advice. Should we be worried about that? The question cannot really be separated from a broader question: how dangerous is complementary and alternative medicine in general? And there is no simple answer.

Some alternative medicine is dispensed under the supervision of medical doctors. That is a good thing, in the sense that it means that there is less danger of an alternative practitioner misdiagnosing a serious illness. But it is also a bad thing, because it shows that CAM has established a foothold in health services and universities on both sides of the Atlantic.

Most teaching hospitals in Britain offer courses in CAM; so do some of America's leading medical schools, including Harvard and Columbia. These courses are mostly designed to teach doctors about alternative medicine as a phenomenon rather than to persuade them of its merits, but the dividing line is a fine one. The nursing profession, too, is branching out into CAM. In America, growing numbers of nurses have endorsed something called 'Therapeutic Touch' (TT), which advertises itself as a form of 'energy healing'. In TT, 'the practitioner moves the hands with the palms facing the recipient at a distance of three to five centimetres. Gentle sweeping movements are employed to activate the energy flow.' Utter horse-shit, as Goldacre would say – and now practised not only in America but also by nurses in the publicly funded National Health Service.[29]

Some alternative practitioners are employed directly by health authorities. Many more are informally linked to the NHS through word of mouth: a doctor or nurse suggests that a patient try aromatherapy or reflexology because 'it seems to work well for some people'. I first heard of cranial osteopathy, for example, when my former GP vaguely recommended it for 'stress'. He couldn't remember exactly how it was supposed to work.

Cranial osteopathy is almost identical to craniosacral therapy; it claims that 'practitioners with a very highly developed sense of touch' can detect a rhythm that pulsates through the entire body and holds the secret to good health. This is, in fact, 100-year-old quackery, dreamt up by one Dr William Sutherland at the beginning of the twentieth century. Orthodox medicine has been unable to find this rhythm; and, indeed, like CST practitioners, cranial osteopaths examining the same patient identify completely different rhythms.[30]

A couple of years after my GP recommended cranial osteopathy, a friend of mine, the novelist Michael Arditti, was nearly killed by it. In 2001, he developed acute stabbing pains at the base of his spine. He consulted a highly recommended husband-and-wife team of cranial osteopaths. They were charming, but firm in their diagnosis. As Arditti wrote later:

> They claimed that the pain was the product of all the negative energy I had stored at the base of my spine. In my enfeebled state, I believed them. Against all the evidence, they claimed to have healed me, pronouncing me free of 'dis-ease' and asserting that the pain, sweats and fevers were simply the negative energy working its way through my body. In despair, I called a doctor who rushed me to hospital, where I was diagnosed with an infection of the spine between the vertebral discs. As the condition had gone untreated for so long, I had developed septicaemia. For several days, my life hung in the balance. I remained in hospital for 14 weeks. I've been left permanently disabled, since the bug destroyed two discs at the base of the spine.[31]

Is Michael Arditti a victim of alternative medicine? Interestingly, he doesn't think so. He remains a fan of CAM.

He says that the fact that he was misdiagnosed by two cranial osteopaths doesn't invalidate other alternative therapies. That would be like damning orthodox medicine because a GP had misdiagnosed the first signs of a heart attack as indigestion (something that has happened countless times).

In my opinion, this is a misleading analogy. When a medical doctor makes a wrong assessment, that is either an honest mistake or a failure to follow diagnostic procedures. Medicine uses a methodology that furnishes doctors with the best available evidence, however incomplete or confusing it is. In contrast, practitioners of CAM can more or less make up their own rules, and its regulatory bodies serve little purpose since regulated counterknowledge is as useless as the unregulated variety. Because Arditti's cranial osteopaths operated in the demi-monde of CAM, it was virtually impossible to sue them for medical negligence.

On the other hand, critics of alternative medicine must be careful not to fall into the same trap as CAM and turn anecdotal evidence into a looming public health crisis. Harry Petrushkin, a junior doctor at St Thomas's Hospital in London, told me that one or two friends of his middle-class parents had suffered at the hands of alternative practitioners. But he added: 'Out of several thousand cases I've encountered professionally in NHS hospitals, I can't think of anyone who was made ill by alternative medicine.' In

2000, a report on CAM by the House of Lords select committee on science and technology suggested that alternative medicine was most popular among the 'worried well'; it also quoted American research showing that the best single predictor of the use of alternative healthcare was higher educational status.[32]

In short, the classic consumers of CAM would appear to be middle-class hypochondriacs. Occasionally they damage their health because they prefer organic snake oil to prescribed medicine, but for the most part it's pretty safe to sniff aromatic oils, munch your way through a bowl of bilberries, or swallow sugar pills disguised as homeopathic medicine. More than safe, in fact: if the placebo effect is triggered, then the effects will be beneficial and genuinely 'complementary' to orthodox treatments.

To grasp the real long-term danger of CAM, we need to return to its central and most objectionable feature: it makes claims that are simply not true. It encourages what the House of Lords report calls the public's 'flight from science' towards a simplistic, quasi-magical world view. There is a natural human tendency to extrapolate fake trends from isolated cases, and CAM exploits it to the full. For alternative practitioners and the lobbyists who write press releases, the plural of 'anecdote' is 'data'. By cherry-picking research findings and twisting statistics, self-appointed health gurus play into the hands of journalists (especially those on the *Daily Mail*) who seem intent on dividing all foodstuffs and medicines into miracle cures and hidden poisons, thereby increasing our tendency to fads and panic. And politicians are gutless in the face of health panics, even when they suspect that 'public concern' (as it is presented) is based on bad science.

The worst example in recent years is the scare over the non-existent link between autism and the MMR (measles, mumps and rubella) triple vaccine given to children. In 1998, the *Lancet* published a paper written by Dr Andrew Wakefield and colleagues describing twelve children who developed autism and inflammatory bowel disease. The paper suggested that the autism might be the result of the bowel problem; it also speculated that, since the bowel problems flared up after the children received the MMR vaccine, the vaccine might have caused the autism.[33]

Wakefield, a lecturer at the Royal Free Medical School in London who trained as a surgeon in Canada, then gave a press conference in which he said that the combination of the three vaccines might overload the body's immune system, leading children to develop the bowel disorder Crohn's disease, linked to autism. He called for single vaccines to be provided for the three diseases because there were 'sufficient anxieties' over the safety of the MMR jab.[34] Professor Raymond Tallis, a former chairman of the Royal College of Physicians' ethics committee, commented: 'To say that this was irresponsible – because the evidence in his paper fell far short of this conclusion – is the under-statement of the century.'[35]

Wakefield's theory has since been negated by several larger and more rigorous studies; the Medical Research Council, for example, examined the vaccination records of more than 5,000 children and found no connection between MMR and autism.[36] Yet it was years before this simple truth could be heard above the babble of concerned parents, alternative health experts, tabloid columnists, celebrities and opportunistic politicians, all of them expressing their opinion that there 'might well be' a link.

As a result of the furore, countless parents held off giving their children the triple vaccine – a decision that had no more basis in science than the refusal of Pakistani parents to vaccinate their children against polio because they believed it was an American plot to sterilize Muslims. In 2002, the mayor of London, Ken Livingstone, advised parents to avoid the MMR jab. 'It seems to me that a child of just fourteen months is incredibly vulnerable,' he said. 'I remember having all these jabs separately – often you have quite a severe reaction. Why whack them all into a child at the same time?' Dr Ian Bogle, the chairman of the British Medical Association, accused Livingstone of 'doing irreparable damage' with this irresponsible statement.[37] Coincidentally or not, vaccination levels in London fell and the incidence of measles rose. As Tallis points out, in rare cases measles is fatal or causes brain damage: an epidemic would kill hundreds of children. In any case, the cost to the NHS of dealing with an entirely avoidable nationwide health scare ran to millions of pounds.

The MMR panic illustrates the downside of the democratization of healthcare. The expansion of consumer choice into medicine is inevitable and often beneficial. People genuinely are empowered by, for example, the release of information about hospital mortality rates, which helps them decide where they want to be treated. It is less easy to say to what extent they benefit from the emergence of a multi-billion-pound market in placebos.

Many doctors would say that, in so far as it takes the pressure off them to treat minor ailments, and also encourages patients to take more responsibility for their own well-being, it's on the whole a good thing. But no one is truly empowered by being given false information about his or her own health. Moreover, there is a difference between allowing consumers the freedom to make bad choices about their own treatment and allowing the boundaries of medical knowledge to be decided by the whims of the marketplace rather than by scientific research. Yet that is exactly what is happening, with worrying implications for Western society and, as we shall see in a later chapter, horrible consequences in the developing world.

5

The Counterknowledge Industry

Some of the brightest and most dynamic people in Western society make a living from counterknowledge. It takes a talented entrepreneur to make a profit from false information, to package it so skilfully that questions about truthfulness and accuracy either never arise or are successfully brushed aside. These counterknowledge entrepreneurs may or may not believe their own claims, but the successful ones all have an instinctive understanding of how social epidemics work. They are not just salesmen: they are what Malcolm Gladwell calls 'connectors', 'people with a special gift for bringing the world together'.[1]

Connectors make friends and business contacts across a wide range of subcultures and niches. They can efficiently spread a message – a health fad or a conspiracy theory – to charities, government, schools, specialist websites and, above all, the mainstream media. If the counterknowledge entrepreneur is lucky, word of mouth takes over and provides free publicity. Imitators jump on the bandwagon.

When this happens, the distinction between producers and consumers of the product begins to blur. Counterknowledge becomes an industry in the broadest sense of the word; it affects not only people's finances and careers but also their personal lives, since access to supposedly secret information can shape the way they think about themselves.

In this chapter, I look at three examples of the counterknowledge industry at work. The first is a specific product: a DVD and book package called *The Secret*, which offers a recipe for achieving material wealth just by thinking about it. *The Secret* became an overnight sensation after it was endorsed by Oprah Winfrey in 2007.[2] It is what you might call hit-and-run counterknowledge: a single fad that will presumably run its course in a year or two. The second example is the mini-empire of the London-based nutritionist Patrick Holford. This is not hit-and-run counterknowledge. Over the past few years, Holford's products and services have become deeply embedded in British society; he is a connector par excellence whose controversial nutritional advice reaches a huge tranche of the public. The third is Gavin Menzies's bogus history book *1421: The Year China Discovered the World* (or *The Year China Discovered America*, for the US market), the creation of which offers us a glimpse into the international counterknowledge industry in full swing.

The Secret was the brainchild of Rhonda Byrne, an

Australian television producer who claims to have stumbled across the 'law of attraction'. This 'law', a version of which was proposed by the self-help author William Walker Atkinson as early as 1906, states that the universe matches situations to your thoughts. 'Like attracts like', so if you imagine a new car, or a new house, or a pay rise, you will get it. On the other hand, if you imagine disaster – bereavement, a burglary, a cancer diagnosis – then that misfortune will materialize. However, once you master the formula, you will find out that the universe is a conveyor belt of presents.

According to the publishers' synopsis, 'fragments of *The Secret* have been found in oral traditions, religions, literature and philosophies throughout the centuries. A number of the exceptional people who discovered its power went on to become regarded as the greatest human beings who ever lived. Among them: Plato, Leonardo, Galileo and Einstein. Now "the secret" is being shared with the world. Beautiful in its simplicity, and mind-dazzling in its ability to really work, *The Secret* reveals the mystery of the hidden potential within us all. By unifying leading-edge scientific thought with ancient wisdom and spirituality, the riveting, practical knowledge will lead readers to a greater understanding of how they can be the masters of their own lives.'[3]

The formula can be summed up in three words: Ask, Believe, Receive. No one knows why it works, we are told, but it may have something to do with quantum physics. At any rate, *The Secret* completely overturns our understanding of cause and effect.

As Byrne explains, choosing an example of particular interest to her target audience, food is not responsible for putting on weight, it is the *thought* that food puts on weight that actually piles on the pounds. 'If you see people who are overweight, do not observe them, but immediately switch your mind to your picture of you in your perfect body,' she advises.[4] And, as your waist size drops, your bank account will fatten. 'The only reason any person does not have enough money is because they are *blocking* money from coming to them with their thoughts,' confides Byrne.[5]

By the summer of 2007 there were 5 million copies of *The Secret* in print and nearly as many DVDs had been sold – and this despite generally dreadful reviews pointing out the obvious: that the law of attraction is a figment of Byrne's imagination. *Newsweek* described her message as ethically 'deplorable' because it implied that even the victims of ethnic cleansing were responsible for their fate. The magazine quoted Professor John Norcross, a psychologist at the University of Scranton, as saying that *The Secret* fell into the 10 per cent of self-help films and books that were actually dangerous. (In the film, a woman claims to have cured her own cancer by using its techniques.)[6]

Unfortunately, the book also falls into the category of titles known in the publishing industry as 'review-proof'

– that is, their following is so strong that no number of bad reviews will dent sales. (The same was true of *The Da Vinci Code*, which is badly written even by the standards of airport fiction.) By the time the sniffy reviews of *The Secret* appeared, the critics' judgement was irrelevant, because, as many commentators observed, word of mouth had taken over.

But what does 'word of mouth' actually mean in this context? The genesis of *The Secret* can be traced back to 2004, when Rhonda Byrne was feeling depressed as a result of the death of her father and problems with an Australian TV series she was working on. Her daughter gave her a copy of *The Science of Getting Rich* by Wallace Wattles, first published in 1910. Wattles was one of a number of turn-of-the-century shysters who claimed to have discovered inexplicable laws of the universe that *guaranteed* financial success to anyone with a sufficiently optimistic mindset. He was a creature of the cultic milieu; but Byrne was impressed, and says his book stimulated her to recognize the 'law of attraction' in the writings of many of today's self-help gurus.

Byrne flew around America interviewing and flattering twenty-two best-selling authors for the television film that became *The Secret* DVD. And it was one of these authors whose publisher persuaded Byrne's publisher, Judith Curr of Simon & Schuster's imprint Atria Books, that the DVD should have an accompanying book. This was duly written, but advertised only within the DVD itself.

The strategy would not have worked, however, if the DVD had not already become a word-of-mouth success, thanks to Byrne's crafty choice of established gurus as interviewees. By recruiting the support of some of America's most relentless self-publicists, Byrne formed a network of formidable connectors. As Curr told *Book Business* magazine, 'We looked at all the teachers [showcased in the book] and added up all the books they had sold collectively, which comes to about 400 million copies. So we knew there were 22 people who would probably be talking an awful lot about this book.'[7]

One of these, Jack Canfield, is the co-creator of the *Chicken Soup for the Soul* series, whose 115 titles have sold tens of millions of copies. After he started plugging *The Secret* on his website, the DVD and book entered the territory known as brand hijacking. As Curr explains: 'Brand hijacking is where the public says, "Just move out of the way. We want this, and we're going to buy it."' New Age centres arranged screenings of the film. Larry King interviewed several *Secret* participants – fawningly, critics said. Finally, Oprah Winfrey took up the title and announced that she had been living according to the law of attractions all her life without realizing it.

The story of *The Secret* will ring bells with anyone who has read *The Tipping Point*. Rhonda Byrne and her colleagues succeeded in turning a marketing campaign into a social epidemic. There is nothing magical about this phenomenon;

as Malcolm Gladwell showed, the tipping point can work just as well for the manufacturers of suede shoes as for New Age gurus unlocking the secrets of the universe. Most of the time it does not work; plenty of authors selling a message just as preposterous as Byrne's have tried and failed to harness the power of word of mouth.

Byrne was lucky. Even so, the success of *The Secret* does illustrate an important affinity between counterknowledge and social epidemics. People who think they have been entrusted with a big secret feel empowered by this knowledge. If they know the 'truth' about 9/11, or the 'real' cause of cancer, or the law of attraction, then they possess information that can change the world. Although the business of world transformation may have to be left to others, they can at least score points at a dinner party. Meanwhile, if the 'message' is sufficiently exciting, their friends will want some of this power for themselves. So they make for the nearest bookshop or health store to hijack the brand.

When we see this happening, it is always worth asking: why is this information secret? Has it been rejected by the guardians of orthodoxy because its implications threaten their own power, or because it is untrue? In the case of *The Secret*, one could hardly ask for a clearer example of counterknowledge. The promise of instant wealth has been a leitmotif of snake-oil merchants down the centuries. And Byrne is not the first 'teacher' to present it in a supernatural context; her law of attractions is a non-Christian alternative to the 'health and wealth' movement among Pentecostal Christians, which preaches that Jesus will reward believers with houses, jobs, cars and relationships. (To be fair, many Pentecostals deplore this Christian counterknowledge, also known as the 'prosperity Gospel', which has a huge following among churchgoers in West Africa.[8])

The Secret brings together several streams of counter-knowledge. Many of the twenty-two gurus featured in the DVD have spread false information or bear the hallmarks of the counterknowledge entrepreneur, such as questionable academic qualifications. 'Dr' John Gray, author of *Men Are from Mars, Women Are from Venus*, holds degrees in 'Creative Intelligence' from the Maharishi European Research University; his PhD is from Columbia Pacific University, later shut down by the state of California for being a degree mill. 'Dr' Joe Vitale was a follower of the cult leader Bhagwan Shree Rajneesh before leaving to create something called 'hypnotic marketing', in which he offers a PhD;[9] his own doctorate in 'Metaphysical Science' comes from the University of Metaphysics, which provides online tuition in, among other things, metaphysical tongue-control technique.[10] Dr John Demartini practises chiropractic, a medical therapy rooted in pseudoscience. Esther Hicks, a New Age author, channels a group of disembodied entities known collectively as 'Abraham'; she and her husband Jerry were in the original *Secret* DVD but had themselves cut out of the 'improved' version after an argument about their share of the proceeds.[11]

For those of the twenty-two 'teachers' who had not already made a fortune out of their products, *The Secret* has offered a fast track from the cultic milieu to the mainstream; from one copy of their book in a New Age bookstore in West Hollywood to a pile on a table at Barnes and Noble. The book and DVD may turn out to be a nine-day wonder, but counterknowledge entrepreneurs are determined to exploit its potential.

Three of the authors, Bob Proctor, Jack Canfield and the Rev. 'Dr' Michael Beckwith (his doctorate comes from the United Church of Religious Science), have teamed up to form the Science of Getting Rich programme, offering books, DVDs and courses. 'You've seen the Movie. Now Live the Philosophy and Claim the Wealth the Universe Has Always Had Waiting for You,' they say. 'Let me be very candid with you,' adds Proctor. 'While many people have recently been jumping on the Law of Attraction Bandwagon, what I am about to share with you is the material at the very core of my success teachings . . . Just ONE LISTEN of these CDs can change everything for you.'[12]

By people jumping on the bandwagon, he presumably means Esther and Jerry Hicks, who claim to be the true authors of the Law of Attraction as transmitted by the 'infinite intelligence of Abraham'. Their decision to opt out of *The Secret* turned out to be a smart one, since in March 2007 their quite separate book *The Law of Attraction* reached number two on the *New York Times* best-seller list. 'You know how an icebreaker is a clumsy vessel designed to break ice?' Jerry (a former circus acrobat) told Robert Chalmers of the *Independent*. 'I see *The Secret* as the icebreaker for the Law of Attraction, which we've been teaching for 20 years. We're cruising behind in our yacht, comfortably.'[13]

Or, to adapt the metaphor, *The Secret* sailed along a river of counterknowledge until it reached the open sea of the mass market. Along the way, it stopped to pick up permatanned motivational speakers, New Age channellers, reverends from unknown denominations and practitioners of junk medicine. These entrepreneurs each had their own followers, whom they were able to point in the direction of *The Secret*.

Crucially, however, the product was presented in a way that enabled it to move beyond these core followers. Its packaging conjured up images of secret documents waiting to be unsealed; hundreds of thousands of people bought the DVD or book because the cover looked intriguing – and reminded them of *The Da Vinci Code*. Like Dan Brown, Rhonda Byrne added a dose of Gnostic mystery to a tired format. Counterknowledge is often at its most potent when it ties together genres and/or conspiracy theories in unexpected combinations.

On the other hand, however many copies it sells, *The Secret*'s appeal will always be limited, by the sheer absurdity of its claims. From the moment it entered the best-seller lists, the book was mocked. *Saturday Night Live* did a skit on it, while plenty of commentators suggested that the fad was being driven by brainwashed Hollywood celebrities and trailer trash ('Secretrons', one critic called them). We might be alarmed that crude counterknowledge could carve out a mass audience almost overnight; but at least there was a healthy backlash.

Far more worrying is a branch of the counterknowledge industry whose connections to the cultic milieu are less immediately obvious, and which feeds off large institutions that lend it credibility – in sociological terms, that reinforce its plausibility structure.

Patrick Holford is Britain's most influential nutritionist despite the fact that (as we saw in the previous chapter) he has no academic qualifications in this field. He is also one of Britain's most influential propagators of potentially dangerous counterknowledge. That does not mean that, by definition, he is a liar or a fraud; it means that he disseminates information that is untrue or that is unsupported by evidence. He certainly seems to believe his own bullshit. The problem is that so do countless thousands of other people.

One could easily devote a whole book to the dubious claims in Holford's oeuvre, so let me confine myself to three specimen charges.

First, Holford circulates misleading information about autism to the parents of children affected by this often devastating developmental disorder. Holford is a supporter of Dr Andrew Wakefield, whose claim that the MMR vaccine triggers autism is unsupported by a single peer-reviewed study; in 2007, he gathered signatures for a petition to stop Wakefield being struck off by the General Medical Council.[14] Holford thinks that MMR may be 'the last straw' that causes autism in susceptible children. He also cites a 'recent review of all the available evidence' that concludes that Wakefield's thesis has not been refuted (which it has); the footnote for this 'review' directs the reader to the website of the charity Food for the Brain (CEO: P. Holford), where it is available only to paid subscribers.

In the section of his website devoted to the causes of autism, Holford writes: 'As with many conditions, there is debate as to whether autism is inherited or caused by something like diet or environment.' This is grossly misleading. The scientific literature shows clearly that, in over 90 per cent of cases, autism is genetic.[15] Holford does not tell parents this, either on his website or on that of Food for the Brain. The latter provides an 'action plan' for parents of autism sufferers which involves giving the children enormous quantities of vitamins and other diet supplements. For more help in 'overcoming autism' – a dubious choice of words, given that autism is incurable and does not go into remission – parents are recommended to visit the Brain Bio Center (Director: P. Holford), whose promotional literature says that 'over several months, most patients spend between £600 and £1,100 on consultations and tests, plus between £2 to £3 per day for supplements'.[16]

Second, Holford has promoted and sold an electronic pendant called a QLink, which is supposed to protect against radiation from mobile phones and laptop computers. As he explains on the manufacturer's website: 'The scientific proof is deeply impressive . . . This revolutionary pendant provides continuous support against electromagnetic radiation via a microchip which resonates at the same frequencies as the body's own energetic field.'[17] Dr Ben Goldacre of the *Guardian*'s Bad Science column saw that Holford was selling QLinks through his Health Products for Life catalogue, and decided to examine one closely by taking it apart.

There was no microchip. Goldacre contacted the inventors of the QLink. 'They informed me they have always been clear the QLink does not use electronics components "in a conventional electronic way". And apparently the energy pattern reprogramming work is done by some finely powdered crystal embedded in the resin. Oh, hang on, I get it: it's a New Age crystal pendant.' Goldacre estimates that the key component of the QLink costs £0.005 to manufacture; Holford was charging £69.99 per pendant.[18]

Third, and most disturbingly, Holford is sceptical not only about MMR but also about the value of vaccination in general. He writes: 'The alternatives to vaccination are to ensure that you or your child has a fighting fit immune system. There is no better way to confer immunity to an infant than breast feeding and, once weaned, ensuring an optimal intake of immune-boosting nutrients. Vitamin A, for example, offers protection against measles and probably polio.'[19]

The suggestion that breastfeeding and vitamins are an *alternative* to immunization is dangerous nonsense. The NHS website for Great Ormond Street Hospital says that no measure, such as breastfeeding or an organic diet, provides better protection against serious illnesses than orthodox vaccination.[20] UNICEF estimated in 2003 that vaccines against measles and influenza could save half a million lives in Africa every year.[21]

Holford goes on to say: 'Although less well researched, you may wish to investigate homoeopathic immunisations. In one study 18,000 children were successfully protected against meningitis with a homoeopathic remedy, without a single side-effect.'[22] He does not name the study; but, since homeopathic remedies contain no active ingredients, it is impossible that any such 'immunization' could protect a child against meningitis. Again, the NHS Great Ormond Street website says there is 'no evidence that any homeopathic remedy prevents those illnesses against which we vaccinate'. Incidentally, many homeopaths draw the line at these dangerous 'immunizations'; Holford's support for them is scandalous – and worrying, since he is extremely well established in the media and the world of CAM.

Holford's best-selling book is *The Optimum Nutrition Bible*, whose publishers, Piatkus, report that it has sold over 500,000 copies worldwide. However, a revised and updated edition, *The New Optimum Nutrition Bible* (2005), has attracted a great deal of unwelcome publicity for him, since it contains the statement that 'AZT, the first prescribable anti-HIV drug, is potentially harmful, and proving less effective than Vitamin C'.[23] Holford does not say in what respect it is 'less effective', but no study comparing the effects of AZT and vitamin C on humans has ever been carried out. Holford repeated this claim on a tour of South Africa in 2007. Ben Goldacre commented: 'I must say I find Holford's claims quite extraordinary in a country with 5 million HIV positive, who have only recently managed to wrestle antiretroviral medication from an HIV denialist government obsessed with using nutritional cures instead.'[24]

Holford is also the author of *Say No to Heart Disease* (1998), *100 Per Cent Health* (1999), *Say No to Cancer* (1999), *Six Weeks to Superhealth* (2000) and *The Alzheimer's Prevention Plan* (2005). Each of these titles reeks of counterknowledge. People who suffer from cancer or heart problems are not ill because they have failed to say 'no' to the disease (the only possible exception being people who have contracted lung cancer through smoking). To imply that chronic illness is the sufferer's fault is cruel and wrong. It is also one of the hallmarks of the quack. There is no such thing as 100 per cent health or superhealth, and the idea that a complete physical transformation can be attained in six weeks merely compounds the nonsense. Alzheimer's is not yet a preventable disease and even to hint as much is also cruel.

In addition to his best-selling books, Holford offers a dizzying range of products and services through his website. For example, for £49.98 Health Products for Life will conduct a 'hair mineral analysis check': 'your hair can reveal much about your inner health,' it explains.[25] No, it can't, says the American Medical Association, which 'opposes chemical analysis of the hair as a determinant for the need for medical therapy and supports informing the American public and appropriate government agencies of this unproven practice and its potential for healthcare fraud'.[26]

Holford also outlines 'five easy steps you can take now to say no to cancer'. Every one of them involves paying money to P. Holford or one of his business associates:

1. Buy *Say No to Cancer* for just £6.99.
2. Join the '100% Health Today' programme for just £49.99.
3. Have a personal nutrition consultation. This can be done online for just £24.
4. Attend a '100% Health Weekend Workshop' – £199 for non-members of Health Today.
5. Follow the 'Say No to Cancer Diet and Supplement Programme', which recommends an Immune Plus Pack of vitamins and antioxidant tablets costing £59.30.

Holford also explains why his programme is so effective: it cuts out the chemicals that he is 'absolutely convinced' are the main cause of cancer. 'Prior to the 1940s these chemicals didn't exist, which may be one reason your grandparents and great grandparents didn't die from breast and prostate cancer,' he says, thereby managing to combine pseudoscience and pseudohistory in one sentence.[27]

Where *The Secret* offered a short cut to semi-respectability for snake-oil merchants, Patrick Holford's mini-empire provides opportunities for extensive and subtle interaction between the cultic milieu and the mainstream. For instance, Holford makes extensive use of a website called NaturalMatters.net in order to spread his message; it was on this site that he defended Andrew Wakefield and asked for signatures in his support. NaturalMatters describes itself as 'the UK's only natural living resource'. It is certainly a resource for the nuttiest elements in complementary and alternative medicine. To pick just one example, it offers a directory of 'colour therapists' who 'use a range of techniques which may include eating foods of a certain colour and drinking water that has been bathed in a certain colour'.[28]

By using NaturalMatters to disseminate his message and products, Holford speaks directly to other counter-knowledge entrepreneurs in the world of CAM and taps into their markets. It makes perfect sense for him to do so: if you are selling useless quack trinkets such as the

QLink, or making medically dubious claims for vitamin supplements, then NaturalMatters offers a ready-made directory of gullible potential customers.

Significantly, however, Holford's contact with the cultic milieu is not confined to run-of-the-mill health faddists. In May 2007, Andy Lewis posted an article about Holford on his Quackometer website, which monitors internet quackery. He noted that Holford's campaigns against psychiatric drugs, his emphasis on vitamins, and his reliance on questionnaires to diagnose illness were all reminiscent of Dianetics, the 'science' invented by the founder of the Church of Scientology, L. Ron Hubbard:

Patrick [like Hubbard] started out studying psychology, and also quickly became interested in how nutrition could help solve mental health problems. This conviction led Holford to set up his own Institute where he could train his followers and also set up his vitamin supplement businesses. L. Ron Hubbard also got into the supplement business too, selling his own multivitamin which he called Dianazene, a mixture of iron and Vitamin C and large quantities of niacin. This concoction was supposed to drive out radiation from bodies and cure cancer. (The Cold War was setting in, and radiation was the scare; now we have mobile phones and Wi-Fi.) Hubbard used the technique of a questionnaire to diagnose 'problems' that Dianetics could cure, an approach that survives as a major recruiting tool today for Scientologists. Patrick is also keen on the use of questionnaires to diagnose mental health problems and the required vitamin regime to solve problems on sites like Food for the Brain and its daughter site, the Brain Bio Center . . .

Patrick has not set up a religion, but he does write books with titles like *Food Is Better Medicine than Drugs*, *Optimum Nutrition for the Mind* and *Mental Illness – Not All in the Mind*. He goes into schools to improve IQ, rid children of mental health issues through providing allergy testing and food supplements, and betrays his dislike of mental health professionals by describing medication as 'mental straitjackets' in his emails to parents. Where Patrick differs most markedly is that he does not tell his followers that psychiatrists are aliens that were present at the dawn of time and have piloted space ships throughout the cosmos to destroy our souls. At least, I can't find reference to this on his website.[29]

Moreover, although Holford is not a follower of Hubbard, he is associated with Scientologists. He sits on the advisory board of Safe Harbor, a non-profit corporation that recommends 'non-drug alternatives for mental health'.[30] Safe Harbor denies any formal connection with Scientology, but it has been accused of acting as a front organization for the church, and its founder, Dan Stradford, is a Scientologist.[31] Holford has also been given a 'human rights award' by the Citizens' Commission for Human Rights, founded by the Church of Scientology to campaign vehemently – indeed, hysterically – against the psychiatric profession.[32]

Why would Holford be given an award by Scientologists? Not simply because he shares their hostility to the 'psychiatric-pharmaceutical alliance', one suspects, but also because he has access to such a wide audience. He frequently appears on television, and in July 2007 was the subject of a segment on *Tonight with Trevor McDonald* in which his Food for the Brain charity was shown testing its nutritional theories on children at Chineham Park Primary School in Basingstoke. The school professed itself delighted with the results of taking pupils off junk food; but serious questions have been raised about the sloppy methodology of the experiment.[33] It seems surprising that a figure as controversial as Patrick Holford should have been allowed to use primary school children as subjects of a 'project' – the word 'experiment' was carefully avoided – however beneficial the results.

Holford's involvement with tertiary education is more formal. At the heart of his mini-empire lies the Institute for Optimum Nutrition (ION), which he founded in 1984 and which has trained around half of all the people in Britain describing themselves as nutritionists (which anyone can). The ION is an independent educational trust which offers students a three-year nutritional therapist's diploma course, billed as 'the longest established and most well regarded nutritional training course in Europe, if not the world'. For the 2007–8 first-year studies, the fee was £3,090, plus the joining fee of £260 payable by all students enrolling on an ION course.[34]

Still, maybe the expense is worth it, for graduates of the course receive both an Institute of Nutrition diploma (DipION) and a foundation science degree (FdSc) validated by the University of Bedfordshire, whose logo adorns the ION website. The ION qualification can be topped up by one year of study at the university (two years part-time) to become a BSc (Hons).

Or, to put it the other way round, a publicly funded university is accrediting courses from an institute run by a nutritionist with no university qualification in the subject who supports bogus immunizations against meningitis, sells bogus electrical trinkets, and thinks AZT is 'less effective' than vitamin C. 'How on earth can an outfit like this be accredited by a university?' asks Professor David Colquhoun of University College London. 'What on earth is the University of Bedfordshire thinking of?'[35]

But surely there is no great mystery here. The relationship between the institute and the university suits both parties. The university does not teach the first two years of its BSc in nutrition (that is, the FdSc course): Holford's institute does so on its behalf. No wonder the university website gives prospective students the telephone number of the ION: that is where their course starts. 'The DipION/FdSc is validated by the British Association of Nutritional Therapists (BANT) and meets BANT's stringent requirements for certification of nutritional therapists,' says the university.[36] That sounds reassuring, though students might be less confident if they knew that nobody on BANT's governing council has a qualification higher than a BSc, and four out of the ten do not have any relevant academic qualifications at all.[37]

Holford, meanwhile, although he has no academic qualification higher than a BSc in psychology, has been made a visiting professor of nutrition and psychology at the University of Teesside. According to a spokesman for the university, Holford was scheduled to take up this appointment in late 2007. He will be attached to the university's Cactus Clinic, whose publicity material says that it uses the technique of hair analysis to identify 'biochemical imbalances' in children suffering from attention deficit disorder.[38] Food for the Brain lists the University of Teesside as one of its donors.[39]

Holford's precise relationship with Teesside was not clear at the time of writing. The arrangement between the Institute for Optimum Nutrition and the University of Bedfordshire, however, has many parallels in the counterknowledge industry. An entrepreneur with a ready-made following offers a product to a business with a huge and hungry customer base. This big player – a university, a publisher, a national chain of pharmacies or a newspaper – realizes that the entrepreneur is driving a fashion that has seized the public imagination; the entrepreneur is keen to exploit the marketing tools and distribution channels of big business. So a (perfectly legal) deal is struck.

In most respects, this deal is identical to any commercial agreement between an independent producer and a wholesaler. The difference is that a disseminator of counterknowledge is dealing in untrue information; he or she is a quack, like Patrick Holford, or a pseudohistorian, like Graham Hancock, or a conspiracy theorist, like the makers of *Loose Change*. The interesting question is: do the big businesses realize this?

Answering this question is easier than trying to work out whether disseminators of counterknowledge believe their own bullshit. In most cases, the businesses *must* know. And if they do not, it is because they have not done their homework. Enter the name 'Patrick Holford' into a search engine and you immediately find several websites dedicated to exposing his junk science. The University of Bedfordshire cannot be unaware of the controversies surrounding Holford, yet it continues to shunt prospective students towards the Institute for Optimum Nutrition.

Likewise, Boots the Chemists employs enough scientists to know that homeopathy is the purest quackery. Yet it continues to sell an enormous range of homeopathic remedies, some of them under its own brand. Anyone who complains about this is told by the customer service department: 'Boots prides itself on offering customers choice and, whilst some people may not believe in the products, a large number of our customers continue to find homoeopathy products beneficial for them.' As Andy Lewis of the Quackometer website points out, 'some people' in this case includes the whole of medical science.

Boots also reminds critics that the government's own regulatory body regards homeopathic products as safe. Hardly surprising, says Lewis, since the pills are made of sugar: 'If they were dangerous, that would be as much of a miracle as if they worked. What is dangerous is Boots giving these pills an endorsement that may discourage people from seeking proper care.'[40] Boots's trade in sugar pills also raises questions about the standard of its in-store pharmacists, some of whom may not know precisely what they are selling. In June 2007, I visited the five branches of Boots nearest my home in west London and asked the (fully qualified) pharmacist whether the homeopathic remedies on sale were actually placebos. One pharmacist said yes; two fudged the issue; two told me firmly that the 'medicine', consisting of sugar pills, was more effective than placebos, and genuinely seemed to believe this erroneous claim. In short, pharmacists trained by Britain's leading firm of chemists were dispensing counterknowledge.

The situation in Boots, where homeopathic voodoo is on sale next to real medicine, is mirrored in branches of Waterstone's, Borders and WH Smith, where pseudoscience and pseudohistory are available adjacent to, or mixed up with, real science and history. When this is pointed out to booksellers, they invariably blame the publishing houses. And they have a point. There is no excuse for WH Smith stocking *9/11 Revealed* by Ian Henshall and Rowland Morgan, a crude far-left polemic published by Constable Robinson that repeats all the *Loose Change* myths and worse; but, for the most part, publishers have played a more active role than bookstores in opening the floodgates of counter-knowledge. The decision to buy in a particular title is often taken hastily; the decision to commission it is taken very carefully by editors who then shape the manuscript according to the requirements of the market, and the media.

A disturbing example of the interaction between a bogus historian and a major publisher was uncovered in 2006 by the Australian Broadcasting Corporation's TV documentary series *Four Corners*. In an episode entitled 'Junk History', *Four Corners* investigated the writing of *1421: The Year China Discovered the World* by Gavin Menzies, which has sold a million copies in over 100 countries. Purchasers include 13,000 'followers' who subscribe to a monthly newsletter available from Menzies's website, a Chinese version of which was launched in 2006.

As we saw in a previous chapter, Menzies, a former Royal

Navy submarine commander, believes that Chinese mariners discovered Greenland, North and South America, Australia and New Zealand in the early fifteenth century. This is a controversial thesis, to put it mildly. Shortly after its publication, detailed scholarly refutations of *1421* were posted all over the internet on websites such as 1421exposed.com.

But to what extent was *1421* really his book? Luigi Bonomi, Menzies's literary agent, admitted on camera that his client was 'not a natural writer', so he rewrote sample chapters from the book himself before sending it out to publishers. Menzies and Bonomi then booked a room at the Royal Geographical Society to announce the 'discovery' of the Chinese voyages to Australia, Brazil, and so forth. 'It was a public relations exercise on my part, to hopefully create a lot of controversy and sell literary rights,' Menzies told *Four Corners*.[41]

Bonomi had another trick up his sleeve. He secured the services of Midas Public Relations, probably Britain's leading PR agency for the publishing industry. The documentary quoted Steven Williams of Midas: 'In Luigi's opinion, it was a bit of a no-hoper as a manuscript and no publisher would touch it. So he had the bright idea of asking us if we could fly a flag and get a story in a national newspaper that would put his theory in the public domain.' The London *Daily Telegraph* (for which I write) duly obliged with an article announcing that 'history books in 23 countries may need to be rewritten in the light of new evidence that Chinese explorers had discovered most parts of the world by the mid-15th century'.[42] (Needless to say, no history books have been rewritten, except possibly in China.)

The resulting publicity, says Williams, was 'certainly one of the biggest stories that we've ever handled as a PR agency. It was just unbelievable.' Bonomi sent out copies of the *Telegraph* article and all the follow-up reports to major publishers. Ten directors of Bantam Press, a division of Transworld, part of Random House, met Gavin Menzies in their boardroom. Sally Gaminara, publisher of Transworld, says she 'wanted to make sure we bought the book before he gave his talk, because if all the other publishers were there they'd all immediately rush to buy the book and the price would go up'.[43] So she offered Bonomini £500,000 for the world rights and he accepted.

Then the production process began in earnest. According to Menzies, Transworld assigned as many as 130 people to work on *1421*, including Neil Hanson, an experienced ghostwriter. But, as *Four Corners* noted, 'strangely, none of the professionals at Transworld who prepared the manuscript for publication was asked to test the theory behind the book'.

Why? 'It's very hard to prove that something is or is not correct,' says Gaminara. 'I mean, we do have to rely on our authors. We simply don't have the time. We work flat out publishing the books, bringing them to press, marketing them, publicizing them, selling them – we can't possibly go through all our books and check every single one of them out for accuracy.'[44]

Maybe so; but is it too much to expect the publisher of the book's US edition to check the accuracy of its five-word subtitle? 1421 was not 'The Year China Discovered America', for one very simple reason: China didn't discover America.

6

Living with Counterknowledge

Credulous thinking is spreading through society as fast and silently as a virus, and no one has a clue how long the epidemic will last. Counterknowledge is not like smallpox, which has been completely eradicated through vaccination. A better analogy would be HIV/AIDS, which has a frightening ability to mutate. No sooner do we think that a strain of counterknowledge is under control than we are confronted by an unexpected variant. Scientific Creationism morphs into Intelligent Design; neo-Nazi Holocaust denial becomes Muslim Holocaust denial.

As a society, we can take prophylactic measures against counterknowledge. Western civilization has developed the intellectual tools to dismantle pseudohistory and pseudo-science. Whether we choose to use them is another matter; the work is hard, usually technical and often unrewarding. There may still be time to turn counterknowledge into a chronic but containable disease. But we are a long way from reaching that stage.

Before we can even begin to control the effects of counterknowledge, we need to understand how the phenomenon developed. It is usually not difficult to follow a strand of information back to the cultic milieu. The doctrines of homeopathy derive from eighteenth-century quackery; Graham Hancock's lost civilizations revive the fantasies of Victorian eccentrics; modern Islamic anti-Semitism draws on the medieval Christian blood-libel and Nazi racial 'science'. But these historical precedents do not explain *why* intelligent people propagate and consume these ideas.

In his book *Why People Believe Weird Things*, Michael Shermer, the founder of *Skeptic* magazine, addresses this question. 'As a culture, we seem to have trouble distinguishing science from pseudoscience, history from pseudohistory, and sense from nonsense,' he writes. 'But I think the problem lies deeper than this. To get to it we must dig through the layers of culture and society into the individual human mind and heart.'[1] The reasons he comes up with are mostly psychological: it is comforting to believe that a psychic can put you in touch with your loved ones, or that eating broccoli will prevent you getting cancer; it is oddly reassuring to know that apparently random acts of evil are being coordinated by a satanic conspiracy. The practitioners of counterknowledge teach us that the universe is not arbitrary, that things happen for a reason.

The problem is that it is difficult to provide solid evidence for Shermer's inferences. A few years ago, I carried out sociological research into Pentecostal Christian ideas about the end of the world. The more I talked to people, the more sceptical I became about broad-brush psychological explanations for unorthodox beliefs. Theories based on mass psychology are not necessarily wrong, but they deal in concepts such as 'disorientation' and 'insecurity' which are hard to measure. What we can do, however, is observe the social processes that create space for counter-knowledge.

Consider the following statistics. Between 1980 and 2005, British church attendance fell from 4.7 million to 3.3 million.[2] Membership of political parties has fallen from 3.5 million in the 1950s to around 0.5 million. The number of weddings in the UK dropped from 480,000 in 1972 to 284,000 in 2005.[3]

Each of these trends reflects the fragmentation of traditional authority structures – churches, political parties and the two-parent family – that previous generations rarely questioned. In the words of Boston sociologist Peter Berger, society is moving inexorably 'from fate to choice'. Modernity and the marketplace dismantle all sorts of institutions, including many whose authority is implicit rather than explicit, such as publicly funded broadcasters and family-run businesses. And every change brings with it new possibilities that are both liberating and a burden.

The subjective side of human experience takes over from the objective.

According to the sociologist Anthony Giddens, we are all being drawn into 'the reflexive project of the self'.[4] The disintegration of communities, the inescapable presence of electronic media, the growing influence of distant happenings on our everyday lives, the bewildering array of lifestyle options – all these factors force us to *choose* who we are, in a way that our grandparents never had to. More possibilities are presenting themselves every day; no sooner have we made these choices than we have to revise them. We are works in progress. And, like artists who present their work in progress to the public, we just love to talk about it.

Indeed, we are bound to talk about it: there are so many things to discuss. It is all very well to be given greater freedom to choose our jobs, sexual preferences, political identity, philosophy and religious beliefs, but in making those choices we first have to decide what we believe. 'The modern individual must stop and pause, where pre-modern man could act in unreflective spontaneity,' writes Berger. 'The answers to the perennial human question "What can I know?" become uncertain, hesitating, anxious.'[5]

Our task is not made any easier by the fact that the public institutions that previously acted as the gatekeepers to intellectual orthodoxy are now telling us that we can believe more or less what we like. Universities, government departments and churches were all hugely affected by the upheavals of the 1960s. As the author of *The Clash of Civilisations*, Samuel Huntington, puts it: 'People no longer felt the same compulsion to obey those whom they had previously considered superior to themselves in age, rank, status, expertise, character or talents. Within most organizations, discipline eased and differences in status became blurred.'[6] This 'democratic egalitarianism' greatly increased the self-consciousness of minority groups: students, ethnic minorities, homosexuals, feminists and political activists. Each of these groups wanted the authority to decide what they believed, including the authority to decide what constituted a fact.

Far from opposing this trend, many intellectual gatekeepers took voluntary redundancy; all points of view (except right-wing ones) were regarded as valid. Institutions founded upon the ideals of the Enlightenment abandoned the very principles that made them. University lecturers across the humanities threw themselves into the task of constructing specialist disciplines, such as black history and feminist literary criticism. From there it was just a small jump to shifting the boundaries of fact in order to avoid offending delicate sensibilities. In 1998, for example, Columbia University Press published *Aliens in America*, a study of the alien abduction phenomenon by Professor Jodi Dean, a leading feminist scholar. In it, Dean refused to acknowledge that alien abductions do not exist and have never happened; instead, she praised the 'UFO community' for challenging oppressive and exclusionary 'norms of public reason'.[7]

There is something appropriate about left-wing academics sticking up for the UFO community, since by this stage many of them were fantasizing as vividly as alien abductees. Scholars created 'narratives' that, in addition to challenging the perspective of a white male elite, shamelessly rewrote history, replacing data with fiction and facts with theory. The transformation of ancient Egypt into 'Kemet' is an example; so are the countless books in the field of queer studies 'outing' historical figures on the basis of zero evidence. And the cognitive dissonance created by this embracing of non-facts was neatly disposed of by the emergence of postmodernism, which sought to delegitimize the very notion of gathering and measuring data.

In the 1980s and 1990s, some French and American postmodernists infected academia with a fantastically pretentious form of scientific counterknowledge. Having decided that science was just another textual game, they started playing it themselves, with ludicrous results. The French feminist critic Luce Irigaray solemnly described $E = mc^2$ as a 'sexed equation' because it 'privileges the speed of light over other speeds that are vitally necessary to us'. She suggested that pure mathematics was biased by its 'sexist' concern with closed spaces, rather than the 'partially open' structures visible to the subtler female mind.[8]

In 1996, the French physics professor Alan Sokal produced a paper, 'Transgressing the Boundaries: Towards a Transformative Hermeneutics of Quantum Gravity', which attacked his colleagues for 'hewing to the "objective" procedures and epistemological structures prescribed by the (so-called) scientific method'. This was just the sort of message that avant-garde literary theorists wanted to hear. Finally, a real scientist had acknowledged that (as he put it) 'the discourse of the scientific community, for all its undeniable value, cannot assert a privileged epistemological status with respect to counter-hegemonic narratives emanating from dissident or marginalized communities'.[9] Sokal's paper was snapped up by the influential American cultural studies journal *Social Text*. On the day of its publication, however, the author revealed that 'Transgressing the Boundaries' was a hoax – 'a pastiche of left-wing cant, fawning references, grandiose quotations, and outright nonsense . . . structured around the silliest quotations I could find'.

The editors of *Social Text* were not amused. Post-modernists may regard scientific discourse as linguistic tricks, but they don't like it when someone plays a trick on them. The consensus among lecturers in cultural studies was that Sokal's hoax was bad form and that his message could safely be ignored. In a 2006 Open University text-book called *Science, Technology and Culture*, David Bell, who teaches cultural studies at Manchester Metropolitan

University, accused Alan Sokal of 'boundary-policing' and 'trampling all over cultural theory'.[10] He wrote: 'Sokal's point was an old one: leave science to the scientists.' Actually, Sokal was saying something subtly different: that if humanities academics are going to invoke calculus and quantum physics, they should know what they are talking about. In most cases, they understand these subjects, if at all, only at the level of popularizations. In some universities, students are being offered two quite separate varieties of pseudoscience: the quasi-scientific theories of literary scholars, and the bogus claims of alternative medicine.

How can universities and other public institutions get away with promoting counterknowledge so brazenly? One answer is that in some respects they are still as powerful as ever. The revolution of the 1960s and 1970s may have persuaded them to surrender many of their traditional responsibilities, but it left much of their internal bureaucratic authority intact. Universities, government departments, local education authorities and publicly funded broadcasters are still run along autocratic lines, though that autocracy is disguised. Their administrators still want to challenge 'elitist' attitudes by promoting 'counter-hegemonic narratives' based on wish-fulfilment rather than data. But, paradoxically, they do so by exercising their own hegemony. And so it becomes official policy to promote versions of history that bolster self-esteem rather than convey useful facts. Passion passes for rigour; counterculture has turned into counterknowledge.

But it would be wrong to blame everything on ageing hippies. Another reason why institutions are able to promote bogus scholarship is that both counterculture and counterknowledge are surprisingly at home in the capitalist free market. The counterculture arose out of modernity, whose main driving force is capitalism. As long ago as 1942, the political scientist Joseph Schumpeter described 'creative destruction' as the essential fact about capitalism. The market is a tremendously radical agent of change; it does not just produce price competition, but also new commodities, new technologies and new organizations that strike at the very foundations of the old system.[11] The middle-class campus radicals of the 1960s and 1970s imagined that they were dismantling capitalism; actually, they were themselves products of a consumerist society, and their narcissistic 'alternative' culture further stimulated consumer demand.

Once people are encouraged to redefine themselves, they need goods and services to help them construct their new identities. Afrocentric pseudoscholarship is tied in to a multi-million-pound race-relations industry that receives massive sponsorship from big corporations. Likewise, as we saw in the previous chapter, would-be practitioners of the new 'science' of nutritionism are batted back and forth between the University of Bedfordshire and Patrick Holford's business empire, paying fees to both.

The free market likes counterknowledge. The troubled newspaper industry – all of it, not just the tabloids – increasingly relies on fascinating but untrue stories to sell papers. Specialist reporters are becoming an expensive luxury; and it is a brave young reporter who refuses to 'follow up' a report that has appeared in a rival publication simply because it is based on sloppy research. In particular, there is nothing like a health panic to boost circulation. 'Dangerous' foods and medicines pose an irresistibly scary threat to the modern project of the self; and, conversely, 'superfoods' offer a secular sacrament of redemption, an outward sign of inward grace. Counterknowledge, unconstrained by inconvenient facts, enables the media to repackage real life into 'real-life dramas' and history into 'mysteries'. Fact is presented to us as entertainment – and, increasingly, though we may not be aware that it is happening, entertainment is presented to us as fact.

It is worth pointing out, however, that many of the most ridiculous non-stories in the press are not invented by journalists but derived from newly published books. The readiness of the world's most distinguished publishing houses to make money from pseudohistory and quackery is particularly sad, since not so long ago these imprints performed the crucial role of closing the gap between inaccessible scholarship and the reading public. Of course, many titles still do this. But these days the presence of a penguin on the spine of a book is no longer a guarantee of quality or even of truthfulness. If people are prepared to pay £10.99 to discover that the northern border of the state of Israel, 33° north of the equator, was decided by Thirty-third Degree Freemasons – one of the claims in Graham Hancock and Robert Bauval's *Talisman*[12] – then Penguin will happily take their money.

The standards of academic publishers have proved similarly flexible. As we noted earlier, the distinguished British publisher Routledge was happy to publish Molefi Kete Asante's *History of Africa* (2007), which does not provide references for its pseudohistorical claims about ancient Egypt. This was not Routledge's first brush with pseudoscholarship. In 2002 it published *Attachment, Trauma and Multiplicity*, a volume of essays edited by Valerie Sinason on the subject of 'dissociative identity disorder' (DID), the new name for multiple personality disorder.[13] Only a quarter of American psychiatrists (and even fewer outside America) believe that DID even exists.[14] Sinason, a psychoanalyst, dismisses their criticisms, just as she dismisses non-believers in the 'peacetime Auschwitz' – her phrase – of satanic ritual abuse. Sinason claims to have 'clinical evidence' of satanists practising infanticide and cannibalism; on closer inspection, however, the evidence consists of nothing more than her patients' 'memories'.[15] *Attachment, Trauma and Multiplicity* contains an essay by Dr Joan Coleman, coordinator of RAINS (Ritual Abuse Information Network and Support), who refers to the 'many' DID sufferers who were 'brought up in families that had practised satanism through several generations'. No evidence is offered for this claim.[16] Coleman also believes that many abusers have 'Masonic connections'.[17]

The reason this *trahison des clercs* matters so much is that, despite the privatization of knowledge caused by the explosion of intellectual choice, Western society still has such a thing as the public domain. Broadly defined, this is a place where ideas no longer carry the copyright of their inventors but are part of our shared culture. The consequences of counterknowledge finding its way into this arena can be very serious. The reason millions of parents have had to worry about the MMR jab is that Dr Andrew Wakefield managed to catapult his batty private theory about autism into the public domain. And there it stayed, thanks to medical professionals, science writers and journalists who failed to expose Wakefield's terrible methodology or publicize the large-scale studies contradicting his claim.

This intellectual sloppiness is more scandalous than the lies and half-truths that politicians tell the public. Indeed, it may even have contributed to a culture of political mendacity. In his book *The Rise of Political Lying*, Peter Oborne argues that the presence of 'shameless, habitual liars at the center of power' during the Blair years was without precedent in modern British politics.[18] Francis

Wheen, attacking Tony Blair in his book, *How Mumbo Jumbo Conquered the World*, for allowing Creationism to be taught in a state school, suggested that the prime minister 'had been infected (however unwittingly) by the cultural, moral and intellectual relativism of the post-modernists, and by the fashionable disease of non-judgmentalism'.[19]

In the final analysis, however, we elect politicians to improve our lot, not to educate us. If we catch them lying about something important, then the punishment is often merciless; but as a general rule we do not take their representations of reality at face value, any more than we believe in the literal truth of advertisements. Most Western politicians do not systematically disseminate counterknowledge; indeed, one of the signs that a politician has left the bounds of democratic discourse is that he deals in pseudohistory or pseudoscience (by, for example, proclaiming the racial inferiority of his enemies). In contrast, we do expect university lecturers, school-teachers, doctors and other professionals to help us distinguish between a fact and an unproven hypothesis.

The methodology of the Enlightenment was under assault from capitalism and the counterculture long before most of us had internet access. But, inevitably, the new medium has speeded up the privatization of knowledge, and increased our ability to incorporate elements of fantasy into our 'work in progress'. Thanks to the internet, millions of people have unconsciously absorbed postmodern relativism. To adapt the old Scientology slogan: if it's a fact for you, it's a fact. And your computer will hook you up with people who share your views, however ludicrous.

Sane people do not normally choose to believe things that contradict the direct evidence of their own senses. You do not decide that you are the president of the United States (unless you are). You may, however, choose to believe that the president ordered fake terrorists to fly two airliners into the World Trade Center. That choice involves, in effect, sticking your fingers in your ears and singing 'la, la, la, I can't hear you!' when anyone points out the falsehoods upon which *Loose Change* is based. Unfortunately, it is also an easy option to take. Just bookmark your favourite '9/11 Truth' websites and join one of Facebook's *Loose Change* groups to link up with like-minded conspiracy theorists. Once again, Professor Jodi Dean is on hand to offer moral support. As she wrote on her blog on 28 January 2007: 'Ultimately, the 9/11 truth phenomena indicate what happens to credibility under the conditions of the lack of symbolic efficiency: there isn't a signifier strong enough to hold together a discourse within which credibility might emerge.'[20]

Andrew Keen, a former digital entrepreneur who has turned into one of the most ferocious critics of the internet, deplores what he calls the 'flattening of truth' in cyberspace. 'Today's media is shattering the world into a billion personalized truths, each seemingly equally valid and worthwhile,' he writes. 'This undermining of truth is threatening the quality of civil public discourse, encouraging plagiarism and intellectual property theft, and stifling creativity . . . Instead of more community, knowledge or culture, all that Web 2.0 really delivers is more dubious content from anonymous sources, hijacking our time and playing to our gullibility.'[21]

The flattening of truth is destroying the critical faculties of young people, says Keen. 'These days, kids can't tell the difference between credible news by objective professional journalists and what they read on joeshmoe.blogspot.com. For these generation Y utopians, every posting is just another person's version of the truth; every fiction is just another person's version of the facts.'[22]

In his book *The Cult of the Amateur*, Keen proposes all sorts of regulatory measures to address the 'democratized chaos' of cyberspace, ranging from legislation aimed at protecting traditional media to moving children's computers out of their bedrooms and into the living room. In reality, it is unlikely that any of these measures would work. Attempts to control the flow of information on the internet are doomed to failure; its infrastructure is simply too complex, and generation Y would enjoy nothing more than running rings around cyber-police. In any case, although middle-class students may be the target audience of manufacturers of internet conspiracy theories, they are not necessarily the people most vulnerable to it.

In the long term, the real menace of the internet is its ability to carry the virus of counterknowledge to societies that are not protected by evidence-based methodology. Take the example of pseudoscientific 'cures' for AIDS in South Africa. For years, President Thabo Mbeki has done his best to hinder the distribution of antiretroviral drugs to his country's 5.5 million HIV-positive citizens; he has described these medicines as 'damaging' and 'toxic' and hinted that the CIA is implicated in the epidemic.[23] In doing so, he has received wholehearted support from Western purveyors of counterknowledge, known as 'AIDS denialists', who dismiss the conclusive evidence that HIV causes AIDS.

The world's leading denialist is Peter Duesberg, a molecular biologist who argues that to prevent AIDS, and even cure the disease, it is necessary only to eat properly and abstain from toxic drugs. The American government's top AIDS adviser, Anthony Fauci, takes a different view, as the *New Yorker* reported in March 2007. After listening to Duesberg speak at an AIDS research conference, the normally mild-mannered Fauci erupted. 'This is murder,' he said. 'It's really that simple.'[24] In the late 1990s, Mbeki discovered Duesberg's work on the internet and subsequently appointed him to a presidential advisory panel.

Mbeki's support for Duesberg opened the door to a whole range of counterknowledge entrepreneurs selling their own treatments for AIDS. One of the most controversial is Matthias Rath, a German physician and vitamin salesman who urges people to take high doses of multivitamins instead of antiretroviral drugs. Patrick Holford, you may recall, is on record as saying that vitamin C is as effective as AZT, though he has never elaborated on this brief statement during his promotional tour of South Africa. The appalling Rath, on the other hand, held a press conference in Cape Town in 2005 at which he stated that 'the course of AIDS can be reversed naturally'.[25]

The South African government, under pressure from the United Nations, is now retreating from its public support for AIDS denialists. But it is doing little or nothing to stop quacks spreading their deadly message; as recently as February 2007, the Rath Foundation helped run a workshop on fighting AIDS at the state-funded University of KwaZulu-Natal.[26] Meanwhile, South Africans in the countryside are slowly gaining access to the internet, where ever more extreme theories are flourishing. One strain of denialism insists that there is no AIDS epidemic in Africa at all. A website called Virusmyth.net links to hundreds of articles written by pseudo-scientists who believe that 'the virus called HIV is harmless and not sexually transmitted; it probably has toxic causes'. At the top of the home page a banner proclaims: 'Support President Mbeki to find the truth about "AIDS".'[27]

The conjunction of modern counterknowledge and traditional superstition in sub-Saharan Africa threatens the lives of millions of people. But it is easy to put to the back of our minds because it has few immediate consequences for the West. The conjunction of counterknowledge and Islam, on the other hand, creates intractable problems both for Muslim countries and for Europe, where the number of Muslims is expected to double from 20 million to 40 million by 2025.[28] As we have seen, the penetration of the Islamic world and diaspora by conspiracy theories and Creationism is terrifyingly high: most Muslims worldwide believe that Arabs were not involved in 9/11; only 29 per cent of British Muslims believe historical accounts of the Holocaust; more than 90 per cent of Muslims worldwide reject the theory of evolution. And these figures are almost certainly being pushed up, not down, by modernity in the shape of digital technology.

Many commentators talk in terms of disaffected Muslim youth being further radicalized by their encounter with the internet. But if we focus too narrowly on 'cyber-jihad', as it is sometimes called, we miss the bigger picture. Islamic culture is unable to defend itself against counterknowledge because it has failed to keep up with the intellectual advances of Western civilization. Pervez Hoodbhoy, professor of physics at Quaid-e-Azam University in Islamabad, has stated bluntly, and bravely, that no Muslim country – not one – has a viable educational system or a university of international stature. 'Although genuine scientific achievement is rare in the contemporary Muslim world, pseudoscience is in generous supply,' he wrote in the *Washington Post* in 2002.

> A former chairman of my physics department in Islamabad has calculated the speed of heaven. He maintains it is receding from Earth at one centimetre per second less than the speed of light. His ingenious method relies upon a verse in the Islamic holy book, which says that worship on the night on which the book was revealed is worth a thousand nights of ordinary worship. He states that this amounts to a time-dilation factor of 1,000, which he puts into a formula of Einstein's theory of special relativity . . .
>
> One of the two Pakistani nuclear engineers who was recently arrested on suspicion of passing nuclear secrets to the Taliban had earlier proposed to solve Pakistan's energy problems by harnessing the power of genies. He relied on the Islamic belief that God created man from clay, and angels and genies from fire; so this high-placed engineer proposed to capture the genies and extract their energy.[29]

Ziauddin Sardar, an influential left-wing Muslim journalist based in London, has observed despairingly that, since the 1990s, Islamic countries have moved away from scientific methodology and towards dangerous obscurantism. 'The Islamic science discourse now follows the way of the Taliban,' he writes.

According to Sardar, Saudi Arabia has been pouring money into attempts to prove that all modern scientific discoveries were foreshadowed in scripture:

> This tendency has spouted a whole genre of apologetic literature (books, papers, journals) looking at the scientific content of the Qur'an. Relativity, quantum mechanics, big bang theory, embryology and much of modern geology have been 'discovered' in the Qur'an. Conversely, 'scientific' experiments have been devised to discover what is mentioned in the Qur'an but not known to science – for example, the programme to harness the energy of the jinn that enjoyed much support in the mid-nineties in Pakistan. This highly toxic combination of religious fundamentalism and 'science', akin to the Creationists . . . attacks anyone who shows a critical or sceptical attitude towards science and defends its own faith as scientific, objective and 'rational'. Unfortunately, it is now the most popular version of 'Islamic science'.[30]

Hoodbhoy and Sardar have taken considerable risks by drawing attention to this assault on intellectual progress by counterknowledge. Yet many non-Muslim commentators consider it 'inappropriate' to make a fuss about what is happening, preferring to concentrate on safer targets such as American fundamentalists. In 2007, W. W. Norton published *Scientists Confront Intelligent Design and Creationism*, a volume of essays edited by Andrew Petto and Laurie Godfrey attacking 'one of the most insidious scientific fallacies of the 21st century'. Nowhere in its 450 pages is there a discussion of Islamic Creationism. Nor is there a single reference to Turkey, the country that is fast overtaking the United States as the major source of Creationist propaganda.[31]

History as well as science is under assault from Muslim counterknowledge. In December 2006, the Islamic Republic of Iran organized a conference entitled 'A Review of the Holocaust' in Tehran, where participants included the notorious French Holocaust revisionist Robert Faurisson and the far-right American demagogue David Duke.[32] One of the attendees was Shiraz Dossa, a tenured professor of political science at St Francis Xavier University, Nova Scotia. In the June 2007 issue of the *Literary Review of Canada*, Dossa attacked the 'illiterate Islamophobes' who had criticized him for going to the conference. Their arguments were based on two fallacies, he said. The first was that President Ahmadinejad had ever called the Holocaust a myth; instead, he had merely questioned its 'mythologizing and sacralizing' by supporters of Israel. Presumably, Dossa had missed Ahmadinejad's speech in the city of Zahedan in December 2005 in which he denounced 'the myth that Jews were massacred'.[33]

Dossa continued: 'The second western fallacy is that the

event was a Holocaust-denial conference because of the presence of a few notorious western Christian deniers/ skeptics, a couple of a neo-Nazi stripe. It was nothing of the sort. It was a Global South conference convened to devise an intellectual/political response to western-Israeli intervention in Muslim affairs. Holocaust deniers/skeptics were a fringe, a marginal few at the conference ... Out of the 33 conference paper givers, 27 were *not* Holocaust deniers, but were university professors and social science researchers from Iran, Jordan, Algeria, India, Morocco, Bahrain, Tunisia, Malaysia, Indonesia and Syria.'[34] Dossa did not say whether he had time to examine one of the exhibits at the conference, brought along by the 'historian' Frederick Toeben, who has served a prison sentence in his native Germany for denying the Holocaust. According to the official Iranian news agency, this was 'a huge model of the Treblinka extermination camp, complete with model trains and human figures, which he said he would use to argue that the gas chambers did not exist'.[35]

Even if we forget for a moment the vile nature of the counterknowledge on display, it is profoundly depressing that academics from so many countries felt that their 'Global South' identity freed them from Western standards of evidence. There is an analogy with conferences on AIDS held by denialist governments in sub-Saharan Africa in recent years; at these gatherings, it was considered unnecessary and even patronizing to subject traditional remedies to rigorous empirical tests. The truth of a claim depended on its provenance and associations, not the evidence of the senses.

The future of global counterknowledge is hard to predict; we could be moving towards a world in which ideological and even religious struggles are replaced, or at least shaped, by battles between real and confected evidence. The endless adaptability of digital technology, coupled with the large-scale migration of populations from Africa and the Middle East to Western Europe, will make such conflicts very hard to contain. Fortunately, however, we do not yet live in a society in which cyberspace has abolished the relationship between public and private knowledge, or globalization has destroyed the relationship between local institutions and the circulation of knowledge. As I suggested at the beginning of this chapter, the West can, and must, take preventive measures against counterknowledge.

One measure in particular springs to mind. In the last couple of years, counterknowledge has proved surprisingly vulnerable to guerrilla attacks from the blogosphere. Freelance defenders of empirical truth, armed to the teeth with hard data, have mounted devastating ambushes on quacks and frauds who have ventured too far into the public domain. The tactic is an antiretroviral rather than a vaccine, and too modest in scope to effect dramatic change in society, but it does seem to work. The lives of celebrity pseudoscientists have been made an absolute misery by

Bad Science, Holdfordwatch, the Quackometer blog and David Colquhoun's Improbable Science website. Reputations are easily damaged in a furiously competitive market, and people rather enjoy the spectacle of smug, rich lifestyle gurus being humiliated.

To go back to an earlier example, if I mention the name Gillian McKeith to my friends, they reply: 'Oh, you mean "Doctor" Gillian McKeith,' wiggling their fingers to signify inverted commas. For that, we once again have to thank Ben Goldacre, whose sustained mockery of McKeith's 'PhD' on his website led one of his readers – 'angry nerds', as he calls them – to report her to the Advertising Standards Authority. As a result, she can no longer call herself Dr McKeith when advertising her products. 'I can barely contain my pride,' wrote Goldacre. 'Is it petty to take pleasure in this? No. McKeith is a menace to the public understanding of science. She seems to misunderstand not nuances, but the most basic aspects of biology – things a 14-year-old could put her straight on.'[36]

Guerrilla bloggers have also managed to focus attention on the incredibly poor standard of science and health reporting across British journalism. By general consent, the worst offender is the *Daily Mail*, which reports implausible 'cures' for conditions such as dyslexia and ADHD alongside scary stories about the electromagnetic dangers of household appliances. But the most irresponsible piece of science reporting in 2007 came from the upmarket, left-leaning *Observer*. On 8 July it led on a story headed 'New Health Fears over Big Surge in Autism'. This claimed that new research had found an increase in the prevalence of autism from one in 100 to one in fifty-eight; that the lead academic on this study was so concerned that he suggested raising the finding with public health officials; and that the two leading researchers on the team believed that the rise was due to the MMR vaccination.

As Goldacre pointed out on his blog and in the *British Medical Journal*, all three claims were wrong. The one in fifty-eight figure was speculative; the academic in question, Professor Simon Baron-Cohen, had made no such suggestion; and the 'leading researchers' were research assistants, one of whom, Dr Fiona Scott, was so convinced there was no link between the MMR vaccine and autism that she arranged for her own child to have the triple jab.[37] The *Observer* was hugely embarrassed by these revelations and removed the story from its website. The *Guardian*, meanwhile, gleefully ran a piece reporting the controversy. (Although the two newspapers are part of the same media group, there is little love lost between them.) On 22 July 2007, the *Observer* finally published a 'clarification'. In it, Dr Scott was quoted as saying that 'it is outrageous that the article states that I link rising prevalence figures to use of the MMR. I have never held this opinion. I whole-heartedly agree with Professor Baron-Cohen that the article was irresponsible and misleading.'[38]

The *Observer*'s reputation for accurate science reporting will take a long time to recover from its flirtation with counterknowledge; for years to come, internet searches for MMR will point readers in the direction of its blunders. That is encouraging. We need a whole generation of digital warriors who know how to damage the professional reputations of institutions and people who propagate counterknowledge.

A good place to start might be the University of Westminster, which received some bad publicity as a result of the *Nature* report into its degrees in homeopathy and other quack therapies, but really deserves to become a national laughing stock. Indeed, so long as it continues to inform students that sugar pills contain magic properties, the word 'University' in its title deserves the same inverted commas as Gillian McKeith's doctorate. The new vice-chancellor of Westminster is Professor Geoffrey Petts, a former professor of physical geography at Birmingham University, who was awarded a medal by the Royal Geographical Society for his work on river conservation. How does he reconcile his own rigorous methodology with running an institution that teaches voodoo science? What does he think a vice-chancellor is for, if not to ensure that his institution teaches facts as opposed to untruths? Let us ask him.

Likewise, respectable publishers who commission works of bogus scholarship should be persecuted mercilessly. What this field needs is its own Ben Goldacre to make the name of Sally Gaminara – who acquired Gavin Menzies's *1421* for Transworld UK – synonymous with bogus history. Then she might think twice before bringing out another ludicrous fabrication, however profitable. She and other senior publishing executives might also be surprised by how little support they receive from junior colleagues. I have spoken to several young editors, including one former copy editor for Graham Hancock, who are privately disgusted by the material they are expected to process. Many bookshop staff feel the same way; I still regret not taking up the offer of a Books *etc.* sales assistant who told me he would look the other way if I chose to shoplift a copy of 'that disgusting trash', *1421*.

We can almost certainly do nothing about the circulation of counterknowledge on the internet. The fragmentation of shared knowledge into personalized truths began centuries ago; digital technology has merely speeded it up. But this inevitable shift from fate to choice does not relieve us of the responsibility to base judgements on the evidence of our senses. On the contrary, it makes it all the more important to preserve the notion of a public domain in which, to quote the *Oxford English Dictionary*, a fact is 'a thing that is known to have occurred, to exist, or to be true'. We must hold to account the greedy, lazy and politically correct guardians of intellectual orthodoxy who have turned their backs on the methodology that enables us to distinguish fact from fantasy. It will be their fault if the sleep of reason brings forth monsters.

Notes

1: KNOWLEDGE AND COUNTERKNOWLEDGE

1 Massimo Pigliucci, 'The Problem with Creationism', in Andrew J. Petto and Laurie R. Godfrey (eds), *Scientists Confront Intelligent Design and Creationism* (W. W. Norton, 2007), p. 22.

2 Ibid, p. 19.

3 See David Dunbar and Brad Reagan (eds), *Debunking 9/11 Myths: Why Conspiracy Theories Can't Stand Up to the Facts* (Hearst Books, 2006), pp. 14–22.

4 *The Conspiracy Files: 9/11*, BBC2, broadcast 18 February 2007.

5 Ed Pilkington, 'They're All Forced to Listen to Us,' *Guardian*, 26 January 2007.

6 For a discussion of AFP's far right links, see <http://www.911review.com/ denial/holocaust.html#hitler>. For the article in which AFP links high-school massacres and Holocaust lessons, see 'Holocaust Education Kills!', *American Free Press*, 18 April 2007, <http://www.americanfreepress.net/ piper/?p=10>.

7 <http://www.barnesreview.org/>.

8 <http://911research.wtc7.net/reviews/loose_change/pentagon.html>.

9 Matt Taibbi, 'The Low Post', 26 September 2006, <http://www.rollingstone.com/politics/story/11818067/the_low_post_the_ hopeless_stupidity_of_911_conspiracies/1>.

10 'Loose Change 9/11 Heading for UK Cinemas,' *Time Out* movie blog, 24 May 2007 <http://www.timeout.com/film/news/1907.html>.

11 Fox News carried a report of the controversy on 29 May 2007. A video of O'Donnell's warm-up comments was posted on YouTube at <http://www.youtube.com/watch?v=hTMB7nM43Sc&embed=1>.

12 These findings come from a national survey of 1,010 adults carried out by the Scripps Howard News Service and Ohio University, 6–24 July 2006.

13 'French Official Suggested Bush Was Behind September 11', Reuters, 7 July 2007.

14 Mahmoud Ahmadinejad, open letter to George W. Bush, 9 May 2006 <http://edition.cnn.com/interactive/world/0605/transcript.lemonde.letter/index.html>.

15 See, for example, <http://www.thetruthseeker.co.uk/article.asp?ID=5099>.

16 Michael Collins Piper, 'Iran's President Speaks Out', *American Free Press*, 9 October 2006 <http://www.americanfreepress.net/html/iran_s_president_speaks.html>.

17 'Iranian Leader Denies Holocaust', BBC News Online <http://news.bbc.co.uk/1/hi/world/middle_east/4527142.stm>.

18 <http://www.911review.com/serendipity/bush_betrays_america.htm>.

19 Michael Shermer, 'Fahrenheit 2777', *Scientific American*, June 2005.

20 Robert Ellwood, 'How New Is the New Age?', in James R. Lewis and J. Gordon Melton (eds), *Perspectives on the New Age* (State University of New York Press, 1992), p. 59.

21 See Tom McIver, *The End of the World: An Annotated Bibliography* (McFarland, 1999), p. 57.

22 Colin Campbell, 'The Cult, the Cultic Milieu and Secularisation', in Jeffrey Kaplan and Heléne Lööw (eds), *The Cultic Milieu: Oppositional Subcultures in an Age of Globalization* (Altamira Press, 2002).

23 See Mattias Gardell, 'Black and White Unite in Fight?', in *The Cultic Milieu*.

24 <http://www.thetruthseeker.co.uk/>, 7 June 2007.

25 Harry G. Frankfurt, *On Bullshit* (Princeton University Press, 2005), p. 55.

26 Ibid., p. 56.

27 For a discussion of the nature of scientific knowledge, see John Hospers, *An Introduction to Philosophical Analysis* (Routledge, 1997), pp. 101–31.

28 Popper set out these ideas in *Science: Conjectures and Refutations: The Growth of Scientific Knowledge* (Routledge, 1963). For a summary of his ideas, and the complex debate surrounding his concept of falsification, see the online *Stanford Encyclopedia of Philosophy* at <http:plato.stanford.edu/entries/popper/>.

29 Adrian Gilbert, *The End of Time: The Mayan Prophecies Revisited* (Mainstream Publishing, 2006), p. 309.

30 Deepak Chopra, *Quantum Healing: Exploring the Frontiers of Mind/Body Medicine* (Bantam, 1990).

31 David Frankfurter, *Evil Incarnate: Rumors of Demonic Conspiracy and Ritual Abuse in History* (Princeton University Press, 2005), p. 189.

32 Jeffrey Victor, *Satanic Panic: The Creation of a Contemporary Legend* (Open Court, 1993), p. 28.

33 Elaine Showalter, *Hystories: Hysterical Epidemics and Modern Culture* (Picador, 1997).

34 Posted to alt.med.cfs on 4 March 1997.

35 Laura Clark, 'Teachers Drop the Holocaust to Avoid Offending Muslims', *Daily Mail*, 2 April 2007 <http://www.dailymail.co.uk/pages/live/articles/news/news.html?in_article _ id=445979&in_page_id=1 770>.

36 'Many Believe Truth about Jesus Was Covered Up', Scripps Howard News Service <http//:www.shns.com> 21 December 2006.

37 For the Nigerian story, see Christopher Hitchens, *God Is Not Great: The Case Against Religion* (Atlantic Books, 2007), p. 45. For Pakistan, see Isambard Wilkinson, 'Doctor Killed as Clerics Claim Polio Vaccines Are Part of US Plot', *Daily Telegraph*, 17 February 2007.

38 See *The Great Divide: How Westerners and Muslims View Each Other*, Pew Global Attitudes Survey, 22 June 2006, <http://pewglobal.org/reports/pdf/253.pdf>.

39 Channel 4 News/GFK NOP survey of 500 British Muslims, 4 June 2007 <http://www.channel4.com/news/articles/society/religion/survey+ government+hasnt+told+truth+about +77/545847>.

40 GFK NOP Social Research, 'Attitudes to Living in Britain – A Survey of Muslim Opinion' for Channel 4 *Dispatches*, 27 April 2006. The survey was based on telephone interviews with 1,000 British Muslims aged over eighteen.

41 'Vatican in HIV Condom Row', BBC News, 9 October 2003 <http://news.bbc.co.uk/1/hi/health/3176982.stm>.

42 'Shock at Archbishop Condom Claim', BBC News <http://news.bbc.co.uk/1/hi/world/africa/7014335.stm>.

2: CREATIONISM AND COUNTERKNOWLEDGE

1 <http://www.kids4truth.com/watchmaker/watch.html>.

2 The US Supreme Court ruling Edwards v. Aguillard, struck down a Louisiana law that stated that Creationism must be taught alongside evolution. For the text, see <http://www.talkorigins.org/faqs/edwards-v-aguillard.html>.

3 Michael J. Behe, *Darwin's Black Box: The Biochemical Challenge to Evolution*, 10th anniversary edn (Free Press, 2006), p. 252.

4 Ibid pp. 42–8.

5 The letter, dated 9 September 2005, was sent under the aegis of

the Elie Weisel Foundation for Humanity Nobel Laureates Initiative. The text was posted at <http://www.pandasthumb.org/archives/2006/03/ _kansas_usd_383.html> and on many other sites.

6 *Science and Creationism: A View from the National Academy of Sciences,* 1999 <http://www.nap.edu/books/0309064066/html/25.html>.

7 'Judge Rules against "Intelligent Design"', Associated Press, 20 December 2005.

8 John Hospers, *An Introduction to Philosophical Analysis* (Routledge, 1997), p. 101.

9 John Dupré, *Darwin's Legacy: What Evolution Means Today* (Oxford University Press, 2005), p. 13.

10 Ibid., p. 15.

11 Robert Ehrlich, *Eight Preposterous Propositions: From the Genetics of Homosexuality to the Benefits of Global Warming* (Princeton University Press, 2003), pp. 51–60.

12 Andrew Brown, *The Darwin Wars* (Macmillan, 1999).

13 Don O'Leary, *Roman Catholicism and Modern Science: A History* (Continuum, 2007), p. 126.

14 Pope John Paul II, message to the Pontifical Academy of Sciences, 22 October 1996.

15 Cardinal Christoph Schönborn, 'Finding Design in Nature', *New York Times,* 7 July 2005.

16 Quoted in *The Tablet,* 5 September 2005.

17 'Vatican Paper Raps "Intelligent Design"', Associated Press, 19 January 2006.

18 For a discussion of the relationship between the different schools of Creationism, see Robert T. Pennock, *Tower of Babel: The Evidence against the New Creationism* (MIT Press, 1999).

19 William Hoesch, 'Flood Geology and Intelligent Design' <http://www.icr.org/article/3192/>.

20 Gallup poll, published 19 November 2004. The figure for 1982

was 44 per cent. Details of the 1982–91 polls were posted on
<http://www.unl.edu/rhames/courses/current/creation/evol-poll.htm>.

21 Alec Russell, 'Children Kept Dinosaurs as Pets', *Daily Telegraph*,
24 June 2006, archived at <www.telegraph.co.uk>.

22 <http://www.kids4truth.com/creation.htm>.

23 <http://creationwiki.org/Main_Page>.

24 <http://creationwiki.org/Mt._St_Helens>.

25 Celeste Biever, 'A Conservative Rival for Wikipedia?' *New
Scientist* technology blog, 26 February 2007,
<http://www.newscientist.com/ blog/technology/2007/02/
conservative-rival-for-wikipedia.html>.

26 BBC profile of Yusuf al-Qaradawi,
<http://news.bbc.co.uk/1/hi/uk/3874893.stm>.

27 Mustafa Akyol, 'Why Muslims Should Support Intelligent
Design' <http://www.islamonline.net/english/Contemporary/
2004/09/Article02.shtml>.

28 Duncan Campbell, 'Academics Fight Rise of Creationism at
Universities', *Guardian*, 21 February 2006.

29 The Opinionpanel study interviewed 1,014 students online in
July 2006. Only 4 per cent (forty-five) of the respondents were
Muslim, which almost certainly under-represents the percentage
of Muslim students studying biological sciences. For the statis-
tics, see <http://www.opinionpanel.co.uk/clientUpload/pdf/
CreationandEvolution(Tables).pdf>.

30 Harriet Swain, 'How Did We Get Here?', *Education Guardian*, 15
August 2006.

31 <http://www.harunyahya.com/theauthor.php>.

32 Harun Yahya, *The Miracle of Hormones* (Goodword Books, 2004).

33 Tom Heneghan, 'France Warns Schools over Islamic Anti-Darwin
Book', Reuters, 2 February 2007.

34 Harun Yahya, *The Dark Clan* (Millat Book Center, 2003),
p. 15.

35 Christopher Knight and Robert Lomas, *The Hiram Key* (Arrow, 1997).

36 <http://www.harunyahya.com/globalfreemasonry01.php>.

37 Matt Mossman, 'Not in Kansas Anymore', *Seed* magazine, 4 November 2006
    <http://seedmagazine.com/news/2006/11/not_in_kansas_anymore.php>.

38 Tom Heneghan, 'Muslim Creationism Makes Inroads in Turkey', Reuters, 22 November 2006.

39 Brian Whitaker, 'The Evolution of Daft Ideas', *Guardian*, 29 May 2007.

40 <http://wordpress.com/blog/2007/08/19/why-were-blocked-in-turkey/>.

41 These figures come from a survey of 4,500 Muslims carried out in the late 1990s by Riaz Hassan, professor of sociology at the Flinders University, South Australia. See Riaz Hassan, *Faithlines: Muslim Conceptions of Islam and Society* (Oxford University Press, 2002), p. 65.

42 'Evolution and Religion: In the Beginning', *Economist*, 21 April 2007.

43 Deepak Chopra, 'Rescuing Intelligent Design – But from Whom?', *Huffington Post*, 24 August 2005
    <http://www.huffingtonpost.com/deepak-chopra/rescuing-intelligent-desi_b_6164.html>.

3: THE RETURN OF PSEUDOHISTORY

1 'Many Believe Truth about Jesus Was Covered Up', Scripps Howard News Service <www.shns.com> 21 December 2006.

2 Dan Brown, *The Da Vinci Code* (Corgi, 2004), p. 15.

3 Laura Miller, 'The Da Vinci Crock' <http://dir.salon.com/story/books/feature/2004/12/29/da_vinci_code/index.html?pn=1>.

4 Ken Mondschein, review of *Holy Blood, Holy Grail*, *New York Press*, 13 July 2004.

5 <http://en.wikipedia.org/wiki/Priory_of_Sion>.

6 The *Timewatch* documentary, 'The History of a Mystery', was broadcast in September 1996. For a full account of the Priory of Sion hoax, see <http://priory-of-sion.com/posd/pdchparchments.html>.

7 <http://en.wikipedia.org/wiki/Pseudohistory>.

8 Stephen Williams, *Fantastic Archaeology: The Wild Side of North American Prehistory* (University of Pennsylvania Press, 1991), p. 33.

9 Dan Brown, op. cit., p. 32.

10 In 1996, the Smithsonian Institution responded to claims that it regarded the Mormon scriptures as a valid source of pre-Columbian information. It put out a 'Statement Regarding the Book of Mormon' which stated that 'Smithsonian archeologists see no direct connection between the archeology of the New World and the subject matter of the book'. See <http://www.utlm.org/onlineresources/ smithsonianletter2.htm>.

11 Laurence Gardner, lecture at the Nexus Conference, Sydney, May 1999 <http://www.magickriver.net/ringlords.htm>.

12 Erich von Däniken, *Chariots of the Gods?* (Souvenir Press reprint, 1990).

13 See <http://www.robertschoch.net/>.

14 For an account of the various rebuttals of the 'old Sphinx' theory, see Paul Jordan, *Riddles of the Sphinx* (New York University Press, 1998).

15 Bart D. Ehrman, *Lost Christianities: The Battles for Scripture and the Faiths We Never Knew* (Oxford University Press, 2003).

16 See Bart D. Ehrman, *Truth and Fiction in The Da Vinci Code* (Oxford University Press, 2004), pp. 158–62.

17 Michael Baigent, *The Jesus Papers: Exposing the Greatest Cover-up in History* (HarperElement, 2006), p. 336.

18 Graham Hancock and Robert Bauval, *Talisman: Sacred Cities, Secret Faith* (Penguin Books, 2005), pp. 481–6.

19 Peter Marshall, *Europe's Lost Civilization: Exploring the Mysteries of the Megaliths* (Headline, 2006), p. 152.

20 Gavin Menzies, *1421: The Year China Discovered the World* (Bantam Books, 2003), p. 456.

21 Interview with Felipe Fernández-Armesto on 'Junk History', *Four Corners*, Australian Broadcasting Corporation, broadcast 31 July 2006.

22 Robert Finlay, 'How Not to (Re)Write World History: Gavin Menzies and the Chinese Discovery of America', *Journal of World History*, 15, 2 (2004)
<http://www.historycooperative.org/journals/jwh/finlay.html>.

23 Speech by President Hu Jintao to the Australian parliament, 24 October 2003, *Hansard*, <http://parlinfoweb.aph.gov.au/piweb/Repository/ Chamber/Hansardr/Linked/2966-4.PDF>.

24 Molefi Kete Asante, *The History of Africa: The Quest for Eternal Harmony* (Routledge, 2007), p. 24.

25 Ibid., p. 35.

26 See Clarence E. Walker, *We Can't Go Home Again: An Argument about Afrocentrism* (Oxford University Press, 2001), p. 54.

27 Molefi Kete Asante, 'Where Is the White Professor Located?', <www.asante.net/articles/White-Professor.html>.

28 Molefi Kete Asante, *History of Africa*, p. 9.

29 Cheikh Anta Diop, *Civilization or Barbarism: An Authentic Anthropology* (Lawrence Hill Books, 1991), p. 92.

30 Mary Lefkowitz, *Not Out of Africa: How Afrocentrism Became an Excuse to Teach Myth as History* (Basic Books, 1996), p. 160.

31 Ibid., p. 7.

32 Clarence E. Walker, op. cit., p. 129.

33 Thucydides, *The Peloponnesian War*, translated by Rex Warner (Penguin Books, 1954), p. 24 (Book 1, Chapter 2).

4: DESPERATE REMEDIES

1 Roy Porter, *Quacks: Fakers and Charlatans in English Medicine* (Tempus, 2000), p. 95.

2 Ibid., p. 94.

3 Ibid., pp. 193–206.

4 Arnold S. Relman, MD, 'A Trip to Stonesville: Some Notes on Andrew Weil', *New Republic*, 14 December 1998.

5 Raymond Tallis, *Hippocratic Oaths: Medicine and its Discontents* (Atlantic Books, 2005), p. 130.

6 Quoted in the FDA Consumer magazine, January–February 2000 <http://www.fda.gov/fdac/features/2000/100_heal.html>.

7 Drugs 'Don't Work on Many People', BBC News online, 8 December 2003 <http://news.bbc.co.uk/1/hi/health/3299945.stm>.

8 G. Ter Reit, J. Kleijne, P. Knipschild, 'Acupuncture and Chronic Pain: A Criteria-based Meta-analysis', *Clinical Epidemiology*, 43 (1990), 1191–9; G. Ter Reit, J. Kleijne, P. Knipschild, 'A Meta-analysis of Studies into the Effect of Acupuncture on Addiction', *British Journal of General Practice*, 40 (1990), 379–82.

9 Jin-Ling Tan, Si-Yan Zhan and Edzard Ernst, 'Review of Randomised Controlled Trials of Traditional Chinese Medicine', *BMJ*, 319 (1999) 160–1.

10 Karen Tye and Karl Zong, 'Bumpy Road Ahead for China's TCM Modernization', *Interfax China*, 4 July 2007, <http://www.interfax.cn/ displayarticle.asp?aid=25517&slug=CHINA-HEALTH-TCM>.

11 D. D. Palmer, *The Science, Art and Philosophy of Chiropractic* (Portland Printing House Company, 1910).

12 <http://www.iahe.com/html/therapies/cst.jsp>.

13 V. Wirth-Pattullo and K. W. Hayes, 'Interrater Reliability of Craniosacral Rate Measurement and their Relationship with Subjects' and Examiners' Heart and Respiratory Rate

Measurements,' *Physical Therapy* 74 (1994), 908–16.

14 Amanda Wynne, 'The Truth About Detox Diets,' British Dietetic Association factsheet, 2004.

15 'No Proof Detoxing Diets Work', BBC News, 7 June 2005 <http://news.bbc.co.uk/1/hi/health/4616603.stm>.

16 'Questions and Answers about Homeopathy', National Center for Complementary and Alternative Medicine, 2003 <http://nccam.nih.gov/ health/homeopathy/>.

17 I am not making this up. See <http://www.mojomoon.net/tleaves.html>.

18 David Colquhoun, 'There's No Remedy for the Prince of Quacks', DC's Improbable Science Page <http://www.dcscience.net/improbable.html>.

19 Michael Baum, 'Homeopathy Is Worse than Witchcraft', *Daily Mail*, 1 May 2007.

20 Statement by Conservative Shadow Health Team on EDM 1240, April 2007. See <http://www.dcscience.net/improbable.html#edm1>.

21 David Colquhoun, 'Peter Hain and Getwell UK: Pseudoscience and Privatization in Northern Ireland', DC's Improbable Science Page, <http://www.dcscience.net/improbable.html>.

22 Jim Giles, 'Degrees in Homeopathy Slated as Unscientific', *Nature*, 446 (22 March 2007).

23 David Colquhoun, 'Science Degrees without the Science', *Nature*, 446 (22 March 2007).

24 Ben Goldacre, 'Eccentric, Brilliant, Bollocks', <http://www.badscience.net/?cat=12&paged=3>.

25 Angela Dowden, 'The Health Remedies in your Fruit Bowl' <http://www.healthspan.co.uk/articles/article.aspx?Id=112&ct=true>.

26 Ben Goldacre, 'The Two Headed Food Monster', <http://www.badscience.net/?p=258>.

27 Ben Goldacre, 'A Menace to Science', *The Guardian*, 12 February 2007, <http://www.guardian.co.uk/food/Story/0,,2011095,00.html>.

28 Ben Goldacre, 'The Truth about Nutritionists', *British Medical Journal*, 10 February 2007.

29 Brid Hehir, 'Therapeutic Touch: Nursing Irrationality?', *Alternative Medicine: Should We Swallow It?* (Institute of Ideas, Hodder & Stoughton, 2002), pp. 30–46.

30 For the claims of cranial osteopaths, see the website of the Sutherland Society, the UK organization for cranial osteopathy, at <www.cranial.org>. For a sceptical view, see Ben Goldacre, 'Cranial Osteopathy', <http://www.badscience.net/?p=132>.

31 Michael Arditti, 'A Very Painful Chapter', *The Times*, 14 October 2006.

32 House of Lords Select Committee on Science and Technology, Sixth Report, 21 November 2000 <http://www.parliament.the-stationery-office.co.uk/pa/ld199900/ldselect/ldsctech/123/12303.htm#a5>.

33 A. Wakefield, S. Murch, A. Anthony, J. Linnell, D. Casson, M. Malik, M. Berelowitz, A. Dhillon, M. Thomson, P. Harvey, A. Valentine, S. Davies, J. Walker-Smith, 'Ileal-lymphoid-nodular Hyperplasia, Non-specific Colitis, and Pervasive Developmental Disorder in Children', *Lancet*, 351; 28 February 1998), 637–41.

34 David Batty, 'The Doctor who Sparked the MMR Vaccination Debate', *Guardian*, 16 July 2007 <http://www.guardian.co.uk/medicine/story/ 0,,2127636,00.html>.

35 Raymond Tallis, op. cit., p. 113.

36 'Study Backs Safety of MMR Vaccine', BBC News, 9 September 2004 <http://news.bbc.co.uk/1/hi/health/3640898.stm>.

37 'London Mayor Warned over MMR Defiance', BBC News, 3 July 2002 <http://news.bbc.co.uk/1/hi/uk_politics/2082344.stm>.

5: THE COUNTERKNOWLEDGE INDUSTRY

1 Malcolm Gladwell, *The Tipping Point: How Little Things Can Make a Big Difference* (Little, Brown, 2000), p. 38.

2 Rhonda Byrne, *The Secret* (Atria Books, 2006).

3 <http://www.amazon.co.uk/Secret-Rhonda-Byrne/dp/1847370292/ref=cm_lmf_tit_1/202–0066898–0763802>.

4 Rhonda Byrne, op. cit., p. 61.

5 Ibid, p. 99.

6 Jerry Adler, 'Decoding the Secret', *Newsweek*, 5 May 2007.

7 Matt Steinmetz, 'The Secret Is Out (of Stock)', *Book Business*, 1 April 2007 <mhttp://www.bookbusinessmag.com/ story/ story.bsp?sid=54064&var=story>.

8 Paul Gifford, *African Christianity: Its Public Role* (Hurst, 1998), p. 335.

9 See <http://www.hypnoticsellingcopy.com/>.

10 <http://www.universityofmetaphysics.com/metaphysical-lessons.htm>.

11 For a survey of the backgrounds of the *Secret* teachers, see Connie L. Schmidt, 'The Wrath of the Secretons', *Committee for Skeptical Inquiry*, <http://www.csicop.org/specialarticles/secretrons.html>.

12 <http://thesgrprogram.com/>.

13 Robert Chalmers, 'The Couple who Claim They Can Make You Rich beyond your Wildest Dreams', *Independent*, 8 July 2007, <http://news.independent.co.uk/people/profiles/article2737966.ece>.

14 Patrick Holford, 'Was Andrew Wakefield Right about MMR, Autism and Allergy?', NaturalMatters.net, 20 June 2007, <http://www.naturalmatters.net/article.asp?article=3203&cat=247>.

15 C. M. Freitag, 'The Genetics of Autistic Disorders and its Clinical Relevance: A Review of the Literature', *Molecular Psychiatry*, 12 (2007), 2–22 <http://www.nature.com/mp/journal/v12/n1/full/4001896a.html>.

16 Brain Bio Center information pack, downloaded as pdf from
   <http://www.foodforthebrain.org/content.asp?id_Content=1721>.

17 <http://www.qlinks.co.za/index.php?p=testimonials&num=6>.

18 Ben Goldacre, 'The Amazing QLink Science Pendant', 19 May
   2007 <http://www.badscience.net/?p=413>.

19 <http://breathspakids.blogspot.com/2007/06/patrick-holford-claims-
   remarkable.html>.

20 'Why Immunise?', Institute of Child Health, Great Ormond
   Street Hospital for Children NHS Trust
   <http://www.ich.ucl.ac.uk/immunisation/ why_immunise.html>.

21 'Millions of Children Dying Needlessly', BBC News, 26 June
   2003 <http://news.bbc.co.uk/1/hi/health/3022558.stm>.

22 <http://breathspakids.blogspot.com/2007/06/patrick-holford-claims-
   remarkable.html>.

23 The relevant chapter from *The New Optimum Nutrition Bible* is
   posted by Holford on his website at
   <http://www.patrickholford.com/ content.asp?id_Content=1793>.

24 Ben Goldacre, 'Patrick Holford – "Food is Better than Medicine"
   South Africa Tour Blighted by HIV Claim', 27 February 2007
   <http://www.badscience.net/?p=374#more-374>.

25 <http://www.healthproductsforlife.com/content.asp?id_Content=
   1617&id_Content_Parent=0>.

26 American Medical Association, 'Hair Analysis – A Potential for
   Medical Abuse' <http://www.ama-assn.org/apps/pf_new/
   pf_online?f_n=browse&doc=policyfiles/HnE/H-175.995.HTM>.

27 <http://www.patrickholford.com/content.asp?id_Content=575>.

28 <http://www.naturalmatters.net/content.asp?cat=81>.

29 'Patrick Holford and Scientology: The Church of Optimum
   Nutrition?', 12 May 2007 <http://www.quackometer.net/blog/2007/05/
   patrick-holford-and-scientology-church.html>.

30 <http://www.alternativementalhealth.com/about/advisory.htm>.

31 Letter from Dan Stradford to Michael Greenberg, 9 February

2005 <http://www.holysmoke.org/cos/safe-harbor-is-scientology.htm>.

32 <http://www.pr-inside.com/three-human-rights-awards-presented-by-r105271.htm>.

33 For detailed criticism of the television experiment, see the analysis by the website Holfordwatch, at <http://holfordwatch.info/2007/07/12/food-for-the-brain-results-on-trevor-macdonald-13-july/>.

34 Institute for Optimum Nutrition, Course Fees and Payment Structure 2007/8 <http://www.ion.ac.uk/ntdc.htm>.

35 David Colquhoun, 'Patrick Holford, the Institute of Nutrition, AIDS and the University of Bedfordshire' <http://www.dcscience.net/ improbable.html>.

36 University of Bedfordshire, Nutritional Therapy (FdSc) <http://www.beds.ac.uk/courses/bysubject/biobiosci/fd-nutthe-iop>.

37 <http://www.bant.org.uk/bant/jsp/bantCouncil.faces>.

38 University of Teesside, The Nutritional Assessment Programme <http://www.tees.ac.uk/schools/SSSL/cactus/nutritional.cfm>.

39 <http://www.foodforthebrain.org/content.asp?id_Content=1604>.

40 For the Boots customer service email and Lewis's comments, see <http://www.quackometer.net/blog/2006/08/boots-quack.html>.

41 Interview for 'Junk History', *Four Corners*, Australian Broadcasting Corporation, broadcast 31 July 2006.

42 Elizabeth Grice, 'Explorer from China who "Beat Columbus to America"', *Daily Telegraph*, 4 April 2002 <http://www.telegraph.co.uk/news/main.jhtml?xml=/news/2002/03/04/nexp04.xml>.

43 Interview for 'Junk History'.

44 Ibid.

6: LIVING WITH COUNTERKNOWLEDGE

1 Michael Shermer, *Why People Believe Weird Things*, rev. edn (Souvenir Press, 2002), p. 275.

2 Peter Brierley (ed.), *UK Christian Handbook Religious Trends No. 5: The Future of the Church* (Christian Research, 2005).

3 UK National Statistics online <http://www.statistics.gov.uk/cci/nugget.asp?id=322>.

4 Anthony Giddens, *Modernity and Self-Identity: Self and Society in the Late Modern Age* (Polity Press, 1991), pp. 4–5.

5 Peter Berger, *The Heretical Imperative: Contemporary Possibilities of Religious Affirmation* (Collins, 1980), p. 21.

6 Samuel Huntington, 'The United States,' in Michel Crozier, Samuel Huntington, and Joji Watnuki, *The Crisis of Democracy: Report on the Governability of Democracies to the Trilateral Commission* (New York University Press, 1975), p. 75.

7 Jodi Dean, Introduction to *Aliens in America: Conspiracy Cultures from Outer Space to Cyberspace* (Columbia University Press, 1998) <http://people.hws.edu/dean/intro_excerpt.html>.

8 Alan Sokal and Jean Bricmont, *Intellectual Impostures* (Profile Books, 1997), pp. 97–113.

9 Alan Sokal, 'Transgressing the Boundaries: Towards a Transformative Hermeneutics of Quantum Gravity', in Alan Sokal and Jean Bricmont, op. cit., pp. 199–200.

10 David Bell, *Science, Technology and Culture* (Open University Press, 2006), p. 36.

11 Joseph Schumpeter, *Capitalism, Socialism and Democracy* (Harper, 1975 [1942]), pp. 82–5.

12 Graham Hancock and Robert Bauval, *Talisman: Sacred Cities, Secret Faith* (Penguin Books, 2005), p. 480.

13 Valerie Sinason (ed.), *Attachment, Trauma and Multiplicity: Working with Dissociative Identity Disorder* (Routledge, 2002).

14 H. G. Pope et al., 'Attitudes toward DSM-IV Dissociative Disorders Diagnoses among Board-certified American Psychiatrists', *American Journal of Psychiatry*, 156 (2) (1999), 321–3.

15 Damian Thompson, 'The People who Believe that Satanists Might Eat your Baby', *Daily Telegraph*, 22 March 2002 <http://www.telegraph.co.uk/opinion/main.jhtml?xml=/opinion/2002/03/22/do2201.xml&sSheet=/portal/2002/03/21/por_right.html>.

16 Joan Coleman, 'Dissociative Identity Disorders: Recognition within Psychiatry and RAINS', in Valerie Sinason, op. cit.

17 Damian Thompson, op. cit.

18 Peter Oborne, *The Rise of Political Lying* (Free Press, 2005), p. 244.

19 Francis Wheen, *How Mumbo-Jumbo Conquered the World* (Harper Perennial, 2004), p. 214.

20 <http://jdeanicite.typepad.com/i_cite/conspiracy_and_complicity/index.html>.

21 Andrew Keen, *The Cult of the Amateur: How Today's Internet is Killing our Culture and Assaulting our Economy* (Nicholas Brearley Publishing, 2007), p. 17.

22 Ibid., p. 3.

23 Michael Specter, 'The Denialists', *New Yorker*, 12 March 2007.

24 Ibid.

25 Ibid.

26 <http://www.ukzn.ac.za/ccs/default.asp?11,62,3,1152>.

27 <http://www.virusmyth.net/aids/>.

28 Robert S. Leiken, 'Europe's Angry Muslims', *Foreign Affairs*, July/August 2005.

29 Pervez Hoodbhoy, 'Islamic Failure', reprinted in *Prospect*, February 2002.

30 Ziauddin Sardar, 'Islamic Science' <http://www.islamonline.net/english/Contemporary/2002/05/Article21.shtml>.

31 Andrew I. Petto and Laurie R. Godfrey (eds), *Scientists Confront Intelligent Design and Creationism* (W. W. Norton, 2007).

32 Tehran International Conference, Review of the Holocaust, 11 December 2006 <http://www.adelaideinstitute.org/2006December/contents_program1.htm>.

33 'Iranian Leader: Holocaust a Myth', CNN, 14 December 2005 <http://www.cnn.com/2005/WORLD/meast/12/14/iran.israel/>.

34 Shiraz Dossa, 'The Explanation We Never Heard', *Literary Review of Canada*, June 2007 <http://lrc.reviewcanada.ca/index.php?page=the-explanation-we-never-heard>.

35 'Hitler of Germany Also Killed Millions of Non-Jews, Conference Says', Islamic Republic News Agency, 11 December 2006 <http://www.irna.ir/en/news/view/menu-234/0612118014175851.htm>.

36 Ben Goldacre, 'Ms Gillian McKeith – Banned from Calling Herself a Doctor!', 12 February 2007 <http//www.badscience.net/?p=362#more-362>.

37 Ben Goldacre, 'MMR: The Scare Stories Are Back', *British Medical Journal*, 18 July 2007.

38 'The *Observer* and Autism: A Clarification', *Observer*, 22 July 2007 <http://www.guardian.co.uk/medicine/story/0,,2132076,00.html>.

Further Reading

The most ingenious, passionate and sarcastic attack on the twenty-first-century march of unreason is by the left-wing journalist and historian Francis Wheen. His book *How Mumbo-Jumbo Conquered the World* (Harper Perennial, 2004) is subtitled 'A Short History of Modern Delusions'. Targets include Deepak Chopra and other New Age quacks, alien abduction fantasists and pseudoscience-spouting postmodernists, all of whom also fall into my category of purveyors of counter-knowledge. But Wheen's canvas is broader, which is both an advantage and a disadvantage. His impressively comprehensive list of 'delusions' comes perilously close to being a list of things he doesn't approve of, such as American foreign policy and especially free market economics, which he portrays as a fantasy almost as dangerous as Islamism.

In contrast, *Why People Believe Weird Things* by Michael Shermer (Souvenir Press, 2002) is more cautious in its choice of 'confusions of our time'. Shermer examines satanic ritual abuse, alien abduction, Creationism, Holocaust denial and maverick science. His focus is mainly psychological; in his final chapter, entitled 'Why Smart People Believe Weird Things', he argues that well-educated people are better able to give intellectual reasons to justify beliefs that they arrived at for non-intellectual reasons bound up with their emotional needs.

Much of the same territory is covered by Elaine Showalter's

Hystories: Hysterical Epidemics and Modern Culture (Picador, 1997). This was the first book to identify the common features of the epidemics of the 1990s. While we may not be entirely convinced by the author's speculation about the hysterical origins of such epidemics, we cannot ignore the startling family resemblances between them. Her thesis is the more powerful because, as a leading feminist academic, she works in the same field as postmodern scholars who lend credence to the genuinely delusional narratives of 'alien abductees' and supposed victims of satanic ritual abuse.

One of the most comprehensive surveys of the American satanic ritual abuse scare is *Satanic Panic: The Creation of a Contemporary Legend*, by the sociologist Jeffrey Victor (Open Court, 1993). He explains in detail how local rumours fed into a wider moral panic fuelled by an unlikely collaboration between fundamentalist Christians and a secular therapeutic culture.

For an English perspective on the same subject, see *Speak of the Devil: Tales of Satanic Abuse in Contemporary England* by J. S. La Fontaine (Cambridge University Press, 1998). Jean La Fontaine is the anthropologist who was funded by the Department of Health to conduct research into allegations of satanic ritual abuse. She found no evidence of such abuse, but she did uncover the horrifying story of how social workers managed to extract fantastic accounts of satanic rituals from suggestible children. A related form of counterknowledge, the phenomenon of 'recovered memory', is the subject of a comprehensive study by Mark Pendergrast, *Victims of Memory: Incest Accusations and Shattered Lives* (HarperCollins, 1998). Pendergrast demonstrates that illusory memories of sexual abuse have been promulgated and validated by misguided therapists, resulting in 'devastating grief and irrevocably damaged family relations'.

Most counterknowledge emanates from the 'cultic milieu', the phrase coined by the sociologist Colin Campbell to describe the social and intellectual margins of society where bizarre ideas can circulate without hindrance. His original essay can be found in *The Cultic Milieu: Oppositional Subcultures in an Age of Globalisation*, edited by Jeffrey Kaplan and Heléne Lööw (Altamira, 2002), together with studies of post-war occult National Socialism, the Swedish racist counterculture, and Satanism in the Italian 'Gothic milieu'.

The historical antecedents of the cultic milieu are buried in a tangle of occult tradition, Gnosticism, folk beliefs, Bible prophecy, early modern conspiracy theories and pseudoscience. The literature covering these subjects is immense. For a picture of the theological ferment at the beginning of the Christian era, see *Lost Christianities: The Battles for Scripture and the Faiths We Never Knew* by Bart D. Ehrman (Oxford University Press, 2003), which examines the patently inauthentic Gnostic scriptures on which many modern pseudohistorians base their claims. *Religion and the Decline of Magic* by Sir Keith Thomas (Penguin, 1973) is a magnificent study of the marginalization of magic, prophecy and folk wisdom after the English Reformation – arguably the moment at which the cultic milieu began to take shape.

Richard Hofstadter's famous essay 'The Paranoid Style in American Politics' (available in *The Paranoid Style in American Politics and Other Essays*, Harvard University Press, 1996) traces the origins of modern conspiracy theories to anti-Catholic and anti-Masonic rumour panics in the early years of the republic. A reading of Hofstadter helps explain the grip that *Loose Change* exerts on the imagination of young Americans. For a thought-provoking recent study of the effect of conspiracy theories on the United States, see *A Culture of Conspiracy: Apocalyptic Visions in Contemporary America* by the political scientist Michael Barkun (University of California Press, 2003). Barkun argues that conspiracy culture is being spread by popular entertainment from its traditional subcultures, the anti-government right and Christian fundamentalists, into the mainstream, where it is rapidly losing its stigmatized status.

The best account of late twentieth-century battles over Creationism is Robert T. Pennock's *Tower of Babel: The Evidence against the New*

Creationism (MIT Press, 1999). Pennock shows how old-fashioned anti-Darwinism has transformed itself into 'scientific Creationism' and Intelligent Design, camouflaging its religious agenda in the process. *Scientists Confront Intelligent Design and Creationism*, edited by Andrew J. Petto and Laurie R. Godfrey (W. W. Norton, 2007), is a multi-pronged attack on the physics, cosmology, mathematics and political strategies of the new Creationism – though, as I noted earlier, none of its sixteen essays addresses the phenomenon of Islamic Creationism. To the best of my knowledge, no non-Islamic book on this subject has been published in English. *Faithlines: Muslim Conceptions of Islam and Society* by Riaz Hassan (Oxford University Press, 2002) contains survey data showing that over 90 per cent of Muslims in Egypt, Pakistan and Indonesia reject the theory of evolution.

Roy Porter's *Quacks: Fakes & Charlatans in English Medicine* (Tempus, 2000) stresses the entrepreneurial vigour of fringe medicine in the seventeenth and eighteenth centuries; the book is even more relevant now than it was when it was first published in 1989, before the emergence of a new generation of ruthlessly self-publicizing 'nutritionists'. *Hippocratic Oaths: Medicine and its Discontents* (Atlantic Books, 2005), by the physician and philosopher Raymond Tallis, contains the most devastating attack on alternative medicine I have ever read; it leaves one in no doubt that the bungling opportunism of health service administrators has proved an enormous asset to purveyors of politically acceptable quackery.

Alternative medicine is one of the manifestations of bad science discussed by the American physicist Robert Park in his book *Voodoo Science: The Road from Foolishness to Fraud* (Oxford University Press, 2000). Many of the counterknowledge entrepreneurs he describes, such as the inventors of perpetual motion machines, might seem like easy targets, and Park's tone is occasionally smug. But his main point is a valuable one: that media stories about fringe science are rarely held to the same standards as stories about politics, foreign affairs or sport. 'Charismatic hucksters' often receive respectful coverage from networks that assign general reporters to cover science topics.

Intellectual Impostures, by Alan Sokal and Jean Bricmont (Profile Books, 1998), attacks a more sophisticated form of huckster: the postmodern humanities professor who appropriates highly technical scientific language which he or she does not fully understand. Sokal, of course, was the perpetrator of the famous hoax; Bricmont is another French physics professor. Their book argues that the left is contributing to 'the demise of reason' by squandering its energies on a meaningless discourse. *The March of Unreason: Science, Democracy and the New Fundamentalism* by Dick Taverne (Oxford University Press, 2005) uses the example of the 'superstitious' campaign against GM crops to argue that special-interest lobby groups and their media allies have created a deplorable mood of pessimism about science and its possibilities.

In comparison with bogus science, few books have been written about bogus history. The most exhaustive debunking has been done by Stephen Williams, a retired Harvard professor of archaeology. His book *Fantastic Archaeology: The Wild Side of North American Prehistory* (University of Pennsylvania Press, 1991) gives dozens of examples of deluded scholars (including Joseph Smith, the founder of Mormonism) who have tried to locate the Lost Tribes of Israel in the Mexican jungle and Vikings in Minnesota. This is the ignoble tradition to which Graham Hancock and Robert Bauval belong.

Not Out of Africa: How Afrocentrism Became an Excuse to Teach Myth as History by Mary Lefkowitz (Basic Books, 1996) is a classical historian's response to the fantasy that the ancient Greeks stole their philosophy from Egypt. *We Can't Go Home Again: An Argument about Afrocentrism* by Clarence E. Walker (Oxford University Press, 2001) is a study of Afrocentrism by a black historian who believes that it encourages black Americans to discard their recent history in favour of a 'therapeutic mythology'.

The social changes that have created space for counterknowledge have been discussed by countless scholars. Chapter 1 of Peter Berger's *The Heretical Imperative: Contemporary Possibilities of Religious Affirmation* (Collins, 1980) sets out the movement 'from fate to choice' which, by undermining plausibility structures, effectively makes heretics of us all. Anthony Giddens's *Modernity and Self-Identity: Self and Society in the Late Modern Age* (Polity Press, 1991) asks how we construct our new identities in the face of almost limitless choice. The effect of the electronic media on this process is described in *Life: The Movie* by Neal Gabler (Vintage, 1998), which suggests that we respond to disorientation by glossing reality and even transforming it into an imaginary feature film starring ourselves. *Mediated: How the Media Shape your World* by Thomas De Zengotita (Bloomsbury, 2005) is a hilarious study of our narcissistic responses to the culture of celebrity. It suggests that consumer choice creates philosophical solipsism; the mediated world flatters us into believing that we are 'above truth', with consequences that are both comic and depressing.